CONDUCTING TRAINING WORKSHOPS

CONDUCTING TRAINING WORKSHOPS: A CRASH COURSE FOR BEGINNERS

Eileen K. Van Kavelaar

Jossey-Bass
Pfeiffer
San Francisco

Copyright © 1998 by Jossey-Bass/Pfeiffer

ISBN: 0-7879-1118-6

Library of Congress Cataloging-in-Publication Data
Van Kavelaar, Eileen K., 1949–
    Conducting training workshops : a crash course for beginners/Eileen K. Van Kavelaar.
      p. cm.
    ISBN 0-7879-1118-6 (cloth : acid-free paper)
    1. Employees—Training of. 2. Training. 3. Workshops (Adult education) I. Title.
    HF5549.5.T7V26 1997
    658.3'12404—dc21   97-33734

Printed in the United States of America
Published by

Jossey-Bass
Pfeiffer
350 Sansome Street, 5th Floor
San Francisco, California 94101-1342
(415) 433-1740; Fax (415) 433-0499
(800) 274-4434; Fax (800) 569-0443

Visit our website at: www.pfeiffer.com

Acquiring Editor: Larry Alexander
Marketing Manager: Matt Holt
Director of Development: Kathleen Dolan-Davies
Senior Production Editor: Dawn Kilgore
Editor: Rebecca Taff

Printing 10 9 8 7 6 5 4 3

 This book is printed on acid-free, recycled stock that meets or exceeds the minimum GPO and
EPA requirements for recycled paper.

CONTENTS

CHAPTER FOUR: CHOOSING AND USING TRAINING AIDS   59

CHAPTER FIVE: MAKING EXPLANATIONS CLEAR   74

CHAPTER SIX: ASKING AND ANSWERING QUESTIONS   86

PREFACE

For nine years I taught an instructor training course designed to enable people to learn to quickly conduct training. My work has been with military personnel from a wide range of occupational specialties—accountants, journalists, personnel officers, computer programmers, recruiters, and physical fitness trainers. The one thing they had in common was that they were suddenly required to be trainers within their respective fields. Many felt overwhelmed. They were unsure where to begin; it's one thing to know a subject, but another to teach it. They had a lot of questions and a lot of anxiety. Most appreciated being able to take an instructor training course.

This is a book for trainers who didn't plan to become trainers and who are unable to attend formal courses. It is written for the person who didn't plan on becoming a trainer to learn quickly enough to get started. The content reflects principles from training literature that I have found to hold true and that I used when teaching the Army's instructor training course. Many people developed the materials for this course over the years and I am grateful for their hard work and the basic outline.

This book is designed to answer the questions I have been asked over and over again by students. Each key concept is linked to one of Aesop's Fables to make it easy to remember. Specific suggestions on how to apply each concept follow its explanation. The writing is deliberately simple and practical.

How to Use This Book

The chapters are sequenced in a way to facilitate planning a training workshop. Each of the first eight chapters contains a planning worksheet. Each time you complete a planning worksheet you finish a major step in creating a training workshop. You assemble the planning worksheets in Chapter Nine, Developing a Lesson Plan, into a detailed outline that describes specifically what you will teach and how you will teach it.

Chapter One, Determining the Context of Training: A Crucial First Step, and Chapter Two, Identifying Learning Objectives, form the basis for all the decisions you will make, so you should read them first. Chapters Three through Seven (Selecting Instructional Methods and Strategies; Choosing and Using Training Aids; Making Explanations Clear; Asking and Answering Questions; and Polishing Communications Skills) should be read next, although the reading sequence is not critical. If you are in a hurry you can skip Chapter Eight, Enhancing Interpersonal Skills, and begin constructing the lesson plan. However, you should read that chapter before you actually conduct the training. Finally, you should also read Chapter Ten, Evaluating Training Effectiveness, before you conduct the training because effective evaluation occurs while you teach as well as at the end of the session.

I'm convinced that if you apply the concepts explained in this book, you'll do a good job as a trainer.

Eileen Van Kavelaar
Indianapolis, Indiana
July 1, 1997

CHAPTER ONE

DETERMINING THE CONTEXT OF THE TRAINING

A Crucial First Step

The Moon and Her Mother

The Moon was invited to a ball and asked her Mother to sew her a gown. "My dear child," said the Mother, "how can I possibly fit your figure? It changes nearly every day. Some days you're a Full Moon; some days you're a Half Moon; some days you're a New Moon. And on the other days, you're somewhere in between!" The only constant in life is change.

One size does not fit all in the world of training. To get the right fit you must consider the context of your training. Three major factors affect the decisions you must make: the learners, the content, and the resources. Think about how these factors apply to your situation *before* you decide exactly what you're going to do. As you read through each of the following sections, make some preliminary notes on the Planning Sheets at the end of this chapter. You will probably uncover some new insights that will influence the way you design your course. You will use these notes later to help you plan your instruction. Note: the first eight chapters end with Planning Sheets to use for preliminary notes.

The Learners

The training you develop must match the background of your learners. How much do they already know about your topic? If you overestimate what they know, they may not be able to learn the material. Learners with little or no background will require a slower pace than those who already have some related education or experience. They also may not be familiar with specialized terms or jargon that you use.

Do you expect some learners to feel anxious about the subject? Mathematics and computer science are two examples of subjects that many people fear. If you think the learners may lack confidence in their ability to learn the subject, now is the time to think of ways you can alleviate their fears. Some ideas follow. See if you can use any of them.

Helping Learners Feel at Ease

If you have taught the course before, *have a testimonial from a former learner.* If the learners can relate to the former learner, they will feel reassured that they are also capable of learning the material.

Tell the learners about any features of the course that may make them feel more at ease. For example, you might tell them their work will be self-evaluated, there is no way they can fail the course, you will guide them through each step, they can work at their own pace, they can redo projects or assignments if necessary, you will work with them individually if they need help, and the like.

Start with a review or overview of important basic concepts. If the learners haven't applied concepts relevant to your course recently, a quick review will make learning easier for them. An example is a review of basic computer skills before beginning a more advanced level of training. An overview provides a summary of a topic before it is discussed in depth. Overviews make it easier to follow complex, detailed topics.

Break down what you teach into small steps and then *give the learners an opportunity to test themselves* after each step. You can then diagnose learning difficulties before they snowball. Frequent checks on learning and immediate feedback should keep learners from getting lost.

Arrange practice sessions so that learners work in pairs or small groups. This way they will help each other. They are often more comfortable asking each other questions than asking the trainer.

Evaluating Learners' Work

Use self-graded materials. If you must correct written work yourself, don't use a red pen! People have too many traumatic memories evoked by red ink. Use a pencil instead.

Don't assign grades or points to learners' work. Adults are very sensitive to criticism in a training environment. Remember that when training relates to a person's job, pointing out an error may be perceived as an affront to competence.

When evaluating a learner's work, *point out what the learner did well,* not just errors. Be specific with any suggestions you have for improvements and don't nitpick. If you point out too many problems, the learner may feel overwhelmed.

Items for All Learners

Regardless of how you answer the questions about the learners, four very important items should be incorporated into your training session. The first three are especially critical when attendance is mandatory.

Begin with an Icebreaker. Icebreakers—short activities designed to help the learners get acquainted with one another—are well worth the time they take. They set a positive tone for the session. People begin to feel relaxed and tend to open up. Nothing is much worse from a trainer's perspective than to have the group sit solemnly in dead silence throughout the entire session. Icebreakers help prevent a stiff, uncomfortable atmosphere. They don't take much time; many can be completed in ten minutes or less.

One well-known icebreaker requires dividing the group into pairs, who then interview each other. The trainer may suggest questions for the learners, such as asking for a brief description of each other's job, hobbies, reason for attending the training session, and the like. Perhaps ten minutes can be set aside for these interviews. Then each person introduces the person he or she interviewed to the group. This is more effective than simply having all the learners introduce themselves. People don't tend to share as much information when they introduce themselves; such an icebreaker does not achieve its intended effect of setting a relaxed, informal atmosphere.

Dozens of creative techniques for icebreakers exist. Consult *The Encyclopedia of Icebreakers* by Sue Forbess-Greene (published by Jossey-Bass/Pfeiffer, 1–800–274–4434) for creative ideas and techniques. Plan on beginning with an icebreaker. It is a critical investment in the overall success of a training session.

Deal with Resistance. If the learners are not attending the training by choice, you are likely to encounter some resistance. Sometimes these or other negative feelings about the training surface during the icebreaker. Getting such feelings into the open is an important first step in dealing with them. This is not the time to act like an ostrich (see Figure 1.1) and pretend that such feelings do not exist. Don't view the fact that some learners would prefer to be doing something else as a personal affront. There's no need to get defensive. That will only fan the flames of resistance. Take the initiative to address these feelings.

FIGURE 1.1. DON'T PUT YOUR HEAD IN THE SAND.

Include a Goals and Expectations Session. A goals and expectations session involves asking all the learners what they would like to gain from the training session. Each learner's thoughts are captured on easel-size newsprint. *It is important that each individual learner be polled.* When everyone's ideas have been recorded, tape each piece of paper to the wall. Usually these sessions take about twenty to thirty minutes to complete. If you have more than twenty-five learners, you may have them work in subgroups, with each then reporting its goals to the class as a whole.

Listen carefully to what the group says. Although you will have a training agenda, make modifications to the extent possible according to what the group wants. If something is clearly beyond the scope of the course, tell the class why that particular expectation cannot be met.

Offer some references to that area if you can. The course content should be clear to everyone from the beginning.

These sessions are a positive way to address negative feelings. Mention the fact that you realize some class members would prefer to be doing something else. You might say something like, "Some of you may be here only because your boss sent you. But since you are here, think about how you can best use this time. Where do you want to start? Where do you want to end up?" Recording their goals on newsprint and posting them in the room shows that you acknowledge learners' feelings and are willing to listen to them. This diffuses a lot of hostility. If you are responsive to your learners and willing to make adjustments based on their needs, they will be more likely to support you in your role.

A goals and expectations session can provide a sense of ownership in the training. Once all of the learners have had their say, tell them what you see your role to be. The success of the course depends on them as much as it does you. You are there to help them meet their goals but you need their participation and feedback for this to happen.

Once the actual training begins, make it a practice to get feedback from the group on a daily basis. Use the goals the group developed as a guideline. Ask if they are getting what they want. Solicit ideas for changes they want to make and then act on this feedback. If the group tells you that it wants to spend more time discussing Topic A, show how you have changed the agenda to reflect that.

Address Administrative Issues. Before the training begins is also the time to define any ground rules. Issues such as start and stop times, smoking policy, breaks, lunch hour, locations of restrooms, telephones, coffee, and similar matters should be discussed. If the group wishes to make some changes, oblige them as much as you can. What difference does it make if they want to change the time they go to lunch?

The Content

The content you teach affects how you can design your course. First of all, who determines the content? Is it the company or organization sponsoring the training? Is it you? Is it your learners? Is it a combination of these? Some situations will not allow you to be as flexible as others. If a company purchases a specific piece of equipment that its employees must learn to operate, obviously there aren't too many subject matter options. In other cases, employees may have indicated on a survey that they would like some training in a particular area. Although you may be an expert in this area, your course will be more effective if you get input from the learners. They probably have specific types of situations that they want to discuss. As a general rule, allow the learners to influence the content as much as you can.

Choose the Right Methods

What you teach also affects *how* you will teach. Specific methods and how to use them are discussed in Chapter Three. Be sure the method or methods you choose fit the type of content you have. If you have a hands-on subject, you will need a hands-on method. Computer training is a common example; learners will not learn without getting their hands on a computer.

If your subject deals with people skills, such as sales or customer service, your learners will need to practice *applying* those skills. They cannot learn only by listening to what you have to say. You will need to set up mock situations where they take turns playing the role of the customer and of the sales or service representative. Also, a people-skills subject requires discussion. This is the type of subject where you can draw upon situations they have encountered to illustrate the ideas being discussed. Even if you have a subject that is solely information-based, such as reviewing insurance claims to see if the customer's policy covers them, the learners need to practice. They will need some realistic sample claims to review. As much as possible, the methods you choose should include having the learners *practice* what they are learning. This often means you will need to prepare fictitious cases or paperwork that mirror real-world situations.

Choose Level of Difficulty

Another consideration in choosing a method is level of difficulty. You will see in Chapter Three that some methods are intended for intro- ductory-level material while others are intended for use at a more ad- vanced level. You can decide on the specific methods you plan to use later. What's important at this point is to realize that your job involves more than just lecturing and answering questions. You must also select and implement activities to involve your learners and give them an opportunity to apply what they have learned.

The Resources

What resources will you need? Be sure to make arrangements far enough in advance to obtain whatever you will need to conduct the training. You may have to alter your plans if you find out you can't get everything you planned to have. Do materials need to be photocopied? Will you give the learners any type of book or reference? What equipment and supplies do you plan to use? Do you need a room with a chalkboard or will a portable easel do? (Don't forget the chalk or the easel markers.) Consider any audiovisual equipment you might use, such as an overhead projec- tor, a VCR to show a tape, or a slide projector. If your learners don't already know one another, use name plates; a five-by-seven index card folded horizontally with the blank side of the card exposed will do.

Think about space requirements. If you plan to divide learners into small groups for a specific learning activity, is your room large enough for the groups to work without distracting one another? Can the tables and chairs be easily moved to accommodate small groups? You may need to arrange for the use of more than one room.

Training Facilities

Always, always, always check out in advance the room or rooms you will be using! You may need to improvise if the room isn't what you ex- pected.

- *Size.* Is the room large enough to accommodate the group? If you are planning to have the group break into subgroups, will they be able to work in the room without disturbing one another? Do you possibly need an additional room?

- *Noise.* Is construction or other noise pollution occurring near the room? If so, is a different room available?

- *Lighting.* How is the lighting controlled? Do all of the lights go on and off together or is there more than one control? This is important if you plan to dim the lights while using a projection screen. If the lights cannot be dimmed, are there window blinds or treatments that can be used? If the room is too dark when you use a projection screen, the learners will not be able to take notes.

- *Temperature.* Is the room too hot or too cold? Can you control the temperature or must a maintenance person do this? If the temperature is uncomfortable, find out what can be done to adjust it.

- *Electrical outlets.* If you are using electrical equipment, is there an outlet near where you plan to place it? Will you need an extension cord?

- *Equipment.* Is everything you asked for in the room? (More than once I've been provided an overhead projector but no screen.) Is it in working order? (Try it!) Is it placed where you want it?

- *Availability.* Are you sure the room is available at all times you plan to use it?

- *Furniture.* Are there enough chairs or desks? Do you have a place to set down your lesson and handouts?

- *Coffee and treats.* Having refreshments on hand helps create a relaxed, informal learning environment. Get them if you can. Check the company's policy about food or drink in the training rooms. Perhaps they can be placed in a nearby hallway if they are not permitted in the room.

Room Arrangement

This particular aspect of the training facilities affects the level of learner participation and communicates either a formal or informal environment.

Auditorium Style. This style (see Figure 1.2) is used for large groups and communicates a formal environment. Learner participation is limited due to the group's size. The trainer is clearly delineated as the focal point. If the room has movable chairs, the group can be broken down into subgroups to allow for more participation.

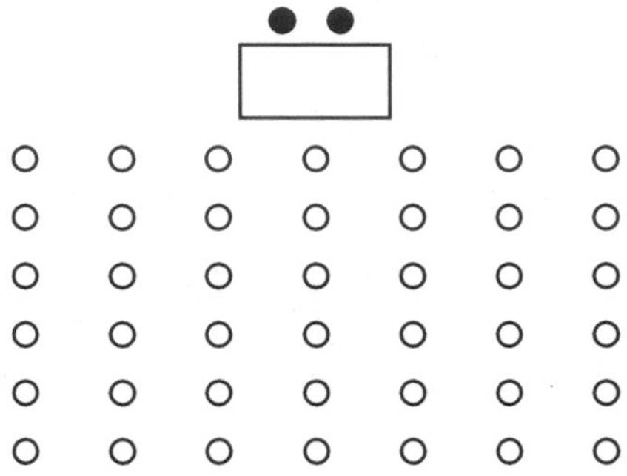

FIGURE 1.2. ROOM ARRANGEMENT: AUDITORIUM STYLE.

Schoolroom Style. Typically used with medium-sized groups (twenty to forty people), this style (see Figure 1.3) is similar to the auditorium style in that the trainer is the focal point and it communicates a formal training environment. The schoolroom style is used with small groups when the use of equipment demands it—for example, in computer training.

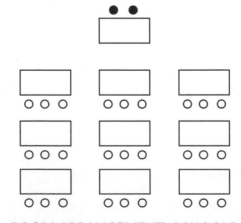

FIGURE 1.3. ROOM ARRANGEMENT: SCHOOLROOM STYLE.

Conference Room Style. This style (see Figure 1.4) is the best choice for a small group. Ideally, each learner can see the face of every other person in the group. The trainer is not set apart as the focal point. The atmosphere is less formal and thus spontaneous participation is more likely.

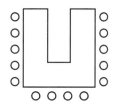

FIGURE 1.4. ROOM ARRANGEMENT: CONFERENCE ROOM STYLE.

A Final Note on Context

Classrooms are very complex places. Context is influenced by many other factors much larger than the three just described. Learners vary by social, cultural, economic, and psychological background as well. Companies and agencies that sponsor training have different missions and different organizational cultures. Each group of learners you teach will have its own personality. A technique that worked extremely well in one group may get a lukewarm response in another.

There are few if any absolutes in the world of training. So before you make firm decisions about your instructional design, make a few notes to yourself about the learners, the subject, and the resources available to you. You will then have a good frame of reference for deciding exactly what to do.

PLANNING SHEET 1: CONTEXT NOTES

THE LEARNERS

Amount of Training/Experience Related to the Topic

_____

_____

_____

Probable Attitude Toward the Training (Anxious, Hostile, Positive)

_____

_____

_____

Possible Techniques to Alleviate Anxiety

_____

_____

_____

_____

_____

Age Range

_____

Gender

_____

Present Position

_____

_____

THE CONTENT

How Will It Be Determined?

_____

_____

_____

Learning Methods

_____

_____

_____

_____

Level of Difficulty

_____

_____

THE SESSION

Icebreakers That Fit Training Needs

_____

_____

_____

_____

_____

_____

_____

_____

_____

Dealing with Resistance

_____

_____

_____

_____

_____

_____

_____

_____

_____

_____

_____

_____

Goals of the Session

_____

_____

_____

_____

_____

_____

_____

_____

_____

_____

_____

_____

Administrative Issues

Length of Training Day

_____

_____

Length of Breaks, Lunch Period

_____

_____

Location of Rest Rooms

_____

_____

Location of Coffee, Snack Machines

_____

_____

Availability of Telephones

_____

_____

Phone Number Where Learners Can Receive Messages

_____

Smoking Policy

_____

_____

_____

THE RESOURCES

Room Availability Secured

_____

Room Size

_____

Room Arrangement

_____

_____

Noise

_____

_____

Lighting

_____

_____

Temperature

_____

_____

Electrical Outlets

_____

_____

Equipment

_____

_____

Furniture

_____

_____

Supplies

Photocopying

_____

_____

_____

_____

Easel/Newsprint/Markers/Tape

_____

_____

_____

_____

Other

_____

_____

_____

_____

CHAPTER TWO

IDENTIFYING LEARNING OBJECTIVES

The Fox and the Goat

A Fox fell into a well. He tried and tried to jump back out but each time he jumped it wasn't quite high enough. Finally, a Goat came by to get a drink from the well. Upon seeing the Fox, the Goat asked, "How does the water taste?" "It's the best I've ever tasted," said the sly Fox, "jump in and join me!"

The Goat jumped in and began lapping up the water. That very moment the fox jumped on the Goat's back and used it as a springboard to jump out of the well. The Goat was now the one trapped in the well and pleaded with the Fox to help him get out.

But the Fox had no sympathy for the Goat. "If you had used your head," he said, "you would have never jumped in without first making sure there was a way to get back out." Having said that, the Fox merrily went on his way. Look before you leap.

Trainers look before they leap by writing learning objectives. A learning objective is a statement of what the learners will be able to accomplish as a result of the training. It answers the basic questions "Why are we here?" "Where do we want to go?" and "How will we know when we get there?"

The main advantage of using learning objectives is that they force you to think about what you are doing and why you are doing it. Their other advantages include the following:

- They clarify the intent of the training.
- They provide a basis for evaluating learner progress.
- They help in selecting the best methods and media for conducting the training.
- They focus your efforts so that you do not become sidetracked.
- They provide a basis for evaluating the training itself.

Contents of the Learning Objective

A traditional learning objective contains three parts:

- an Action
- a Condition under which the Action will be performed
- a Standard of acceptable performance

For example: Identify the bones of the skeletal system (action) by using an unlabeled diagram (condition); name at least 185 of the bones correctly (standard).

Action

The action part of an objective specifies the outcome of the training; it is a statement of what the learner will be able to do at the end of the training. The action clarifies the overall intent of the training. Action statements are specifically worded so that they are not open to a wide range of interpretation. Action verbs such as *write, solve,* and *identify* communicate the intent of the training more clearly than words such as *know, understand,* or *appreciate.* In the example just given, stating that the learner must be able to identify the bones of the skeletal system communicates the learning outcome more clearly than "have a good understanding of the skeletal system."

Sometimes the intent of the training is obvious, especially when teaching a skill. Learners enrolled in a course to learn how to type can reasonably assume that they should know how to type by the end of the course. However, some subjects are not so easily defined. People-skills courses, such as on interpersonal communications or customer relations, could be interpreted in different ways. Expectations of what will be accomplished in this type of training may vary widely. You as the trainer will have some tentative objectives in mind but your learners may have other ideas that hadn't occurred to you. Often you will be able to incorporate specific issues that are important to the learners. Allowing them to modify the objectives to match their learning needs ensures that the training is meaningful and relevant. A discussion of what the course will entail should take place during the goals and expectations session (described in Chapter One). When you are not in a position to modify the objectives, at least learners know what to expect. Those who wanted something quite different from what you had planned may be able to withdraw before wasting a significant amount of time.

The next two parts of a learning objective are useful if you must formally evaluate the learners on an individual basis. Some types of training require certifying that individuals are competent. When you are in the position of having to attest to a specific competence level, the learners should be informed *exactly* how they will be evaluated. They should be told both the conditions under which they will be evaluated and the standards of acceptable performance.

Conditions

The Conditions portion of a learning objective answers the question "Under what conditions will the test be taken?" It describes the testing environment. Conditions either state what a learner will be *provided* or what a learner will be *denied*. Typical conditions stating what a learner will be provided include the references and equipment the learner is allowed to use during the test or evaluation. For example, learners being evaluated on ability to solve mathematics problems may be told that they will be allowed to use calculators during the test; learners giving a speech may be told that they will be allowed to use notes. A condition that deliberately denies the learner access to something often is worded "without references" or "from memory." There should be a justifiable reason any time a learner is required to perform a task without the use of references. The conditions of the testing environment should approximate the work environment. If a learner will have access to a certain reference on the job, it probably does not make sense to deny access to that reference during the test. However, tasks that must be performed quickly or in life-threatening situations can reasonably be tested without allowing references. Many medical tasks fall into this category.

Standards

The Standards portion of a learning objective refers to how well the learner must perform or what criteria will be used to determine if the learner's performance is acceptable. Standards vary according to the type of task. Common standards include speed, accuracy, quality of a finished product, and written guidelines. A typing course may have standards stating that the learner must type at least thirty-five words per minute (speed) with no more than five errors (accuracy) in order to pass. A possible standard for a photography course is for processed film to be free of blemishes (quality of finished product). Those learning to repair computers may be told they must follow the instructions contained in a repair manual (written guidelines). The instructor of a public speaking course may use criteria such as vocal inflection, eye contact, use of gestures, and grammar to evaluate individual speeches.

The reason for stating conditions and standards is to ensure that a test or other means of evaluation does not come as a surprise to the learners. If you must formally evaluate learners' work, it's only fair to tell them from the start how this will be done.

Exceptions

Not all learning objectives need stated conditions and standards. You must consider the learners' background and the context in which you are teaching. The purpose of a learning objective is to clearly communicate the intent of the learning. A learning objective that unnecessarily limits the scope of the training or that is used to meet the needs of the trainer as opposed to the needs of the learners is not very helpful. Training sessions that allow learners to establish their own agenda or that are solely for self-enrichment do not need conditions and standards.

For example, if you were conducting a workshop on the topic "Planning a Career Transition," how could you evaluate a person's decision to move from career A to career B? It would be unethical for you to attempt to do so! Although the intent may be for the participants to choose a career that they find rewarding, only time will tell if an individual's decision is in fact wise. However, to state a measurable learning objective, such as "You should be able to list from memory at least five criteria to consider when planning a new career," does not reflect the scope of what you want to achieve and sounds artificial. The point is that learning objectives should be appropriate for the context in which you are teaching.

The main advantage of using learning objectives is that they force you to think about what you are doing and why you are doing it. When learners can be involved in planning or modifying course objectives, they gain a sense of ownership in the training and will probably perceive it as relevant. Even if the objectives cannot be negotiated, the learners will appreciate knowing what to expect from the course.

Methods and Media

Learning objectives also lay the groundwork for selecting instructional methods and media. Methods and media cannot be evaluated outside the context in which they will be used. They should make sense for the type of objective being learned. If you were training salespersons to overcome possible customer objections, using a role-play method in which the learners take turns playing the role of both the salesperson and the customer is a better choice than lecturing on the subject. A videotape of an effective sales transaction would be a better choice of media than an audiotape of the same transaction. Chapters Three and Four discuss how to choose appropriate instructional methods and media for different types of objectives.

Do not toss the learning objectives aside once the training begins. Use them as guideposts to monitor what's happening. Perhaps you notice that the class wants to spend a good deal of time discussing a topic unrelated to the course objectives. Depending on the situation, this could be a time to reevaluate the original objectives or a cue for you to diplomatically refocus attention on them. Or perhaps you realize the objectives are not being met because the learners do not have as much background in the subject as you supposed. If the original learning objectives turn out to be unrealistic, they should be modified—especially if you must formally evaluate the learners!

Finally, at the end of the training, ask the learners if they think the objectives were met. Use their feedback for future planning.

PLANNING SHEET 2: LEARNING OBJECTIVES

Learning Objectives for the Training Session

LEARNING OBJECTIVE 1

Action

_____

_____

_____

Conditions

_____

_____

_____

Standard

_____

_____

_____

LEARNING OBJECTIVE 2

Action

_____

_____

_____

Conditions

_____

_____

_____

Standard

_____

_____

_____

LEARNING OBJECTIVE 3

Action

_____

_____

_____

Conditions

_____

_____

_____

Standard

_____

_____

_____

CHAPTER THREE

SELECTING INSTRUCTIONAL METHODS AND STRATEGIES

The Farmer and His Sons

A rich old farmer, who was dying, asked his sons to gather around him. "The time has come for me to reveal a family secret," he said. "Somewhere on our land is a hidden treasure. Although I do not know exactly where it is buried, I have no doubt that it is there. You must under no circumstances sell our land. Give me your word that you will turn over every inch of ground until you find the treasure."

The sons granted their father his last request. The day after he was buried, they began digging in search of the treasure. Not one inch was left unturned. As thorough as their search had been, they never found any hidden gold or jewels.

But at harvest time their farm, with its earth so thoroughly worked, reaped the highest profit in the village. They then realized that the treasure their father had referred to was a bountiful harvest. In their industry, they found the treasure.

One of the most-emphasized principles of effective training is to get people actively involved. The treasure of learning is in the joy of discovery, and this is something learners must do for themselves. Conducting a class should not amount to giving a speech! There are several reasons why oftentimes the learners should do as much talking (if not more) than you:

- It gives them ownership in the class—the class becomes theirs, not yours.
- The class will be more relevant to them if they can relate experiences they have had pertaining to the subject.
- They are more likely to remain interested. It's very difficult to listen to just one person speak for more than a few minutes without tuning out.
- You will get feedback on how well they are comprehending the material.

Even if you are teaching a subject that does not lend itself to discussion, such as the procedure for operating a machine, there are still methods and strategies you can use to keep the learners involved.

Methods, Strategies, and Techniques

An instructional *method* is a way of presenting subject matter to learners. It has steps to follow. An instructional *strategy* is a specific procedure used to supplement a method. It is much simpler than a method and is used for a shorter period of time. An instructional *technique* is a specific action taken by the trainer that helps to implement the method. Techniques can be verbal or nonverbal. Examples of verbal techniques include asking open-ended questions, giving directions, and complimenting good work. Examples of nonverbal techniques are smiling, moving toward a learner who is asking a question, and remaining silent while learners contemplate a question. This chapter describes fourteen instructional methods and five instructional strategies. Instructional techniques are mentioned when they apply to a particular method or strategy.

The instructional methods and strategies in this chapter are basic models. You can change them in countless ways. No single method will match the needs of every possible learning situation. Nor is any one intrinsically superior to another. A method is either appropriate or not for a given situation. When selecting a method, consider the following.

The Subject

The methods you choose must fit the type of subject matter being taught. Some subjects lend themselves to more choices of methods than others; a class on filling out insurance forms will have fewer than a class on dealing with irate customers. The method you choose should simulate the real world environment where the learners will apply the training. Therefore a class on completing insurance forms should include having learners practice this task; a class on dealing with irate customers should include some realistic situations that learners can practice resolving. A class on how to use a specific type of equipment must actually have the equipment on hand for demonstration and practice.

Class Size

Some methods are best suited for small groups (twenty or fewer learners). If you have a large group, you will have to divide the class into smaller groups to get everyone involved. For example, you may have a subject that lends itself to a discussion but find yourself with a group of forty people. You could divide the class into small groups and have each group discuss the topic.

Large classes also don't lend themselves to one-on-one instruction. Perhaps you want to play the role of an irate customer and have each learner practice dealing with you effectively. You would have to modify this idea if you had a large class. Again, the class could be broken into small groups and learners could take turns playing both the role of the irate customer and of the customer relations employee. Another alternative would be to have a few learners play the role with you in front of the entire group.

Resources

Two key resources to consider when selecting methods and strategies are *time* and *space*. Some methods are more time-consuming than others. The more actively involved the learners are, the more time you will need. When planning a training agenda, you must allow time for the learners' involvement. For example, discussion of a topic takes longer than a lecture about it. Methods that require learners to work on a task in small groups often are more time-consuming than having the learners independently complete the same task, because a group must first agree on how to proceed. Small-group work also requires that each group report on its completed task or activity. If the class were divided into four small groups to discuss ways to deal with irate customers, each should explain its ideas to the entire class. You must allow time for this when planning a training agenda.

Having learners practice a task requires additional time. Most hands-on tasks require supervised practice so that learners can get help if they need it. For example, learning how to use a computer to produce graphs and charts requires time to practice constructing them. This time must be incorporated into your training agenda.

Also, many hands-on tasks require that you watch each learner perform the task. For example, people learning CPR must be observed individually to ensure they are correctly applying the procedures. If you have a large group, see if you can arrange to have additional trainers available to assist when it is time to check individual progress on the task.

Additional space requirements come into play anytime you divide the class into small groups. Each group should be able to conduct its task or discussion undistracted by conversations in other groups. In some instances, groups may need to move to other rooms in order to work without being disturbed. A related requirement may be movable tables and chairs.

The Learners

The amount of background the learners already have on the subject should affect the choice of method. Some methods are best used with learners who have little or no background; others are geared toward learners who have an extensive background. The methods described in the following sections indicate the required level of subject matter background. Many of the more interesting methods are, in their true form, intended for advanced-level training. However, you can often modify these methods to suit your situation. Even if you are teaching an introductory-level course, you can move to intermediate-level methods once your learners have acquired some background through classes or reading.

Introductory-Level Instructional Methods

Use the following three methods when learners have no background knowledge related to the content of the training.

Lecture

A lecture is a prepared talk used to present information. The learners' attention is focused on the trainer. It is a passive method of learning where the learners listen while the trainer speaks. The learners are not required to participate in any way.

Lectures have limitations. They can quickly become boring for the learners. It's difficult to remain attentive when only one person is talking for an extended time. Also, there is no feedback; the trainer doesn't know if the learners are comprehending the material and the learners don't know if they are interpreting the material correctly. Hint: avoid using lecture as the sole method of instruction. If you must lecture, supplement it with a strategy to get learners actively involved. Move on to an intermediate method once learners have acquired some background knowledge. Note: the advanced methods listed in this chapter can be modified for use at the intermediate level.

Steps

- The trainer introduces the subject.
- The trainer presents the information.
- The trainer summarizes the material and concludes with a closing statement emphasizing the importance of the subject.

Note: some of the following complementary methods and strategies may be unfamiliar to you at first reading, but don't worry; all of them are defined by chapter's end.

Complementary Methods

- *Independent practice*—allows learners to apply concepts taught in the lecture and can reinforce learning
- *Study assignment*—provides background knowledge or a frame of reference for putting new concepts into context

Complementary Strategies

- *Buzz session*—to have learners discuss an aspect of the subject in small groups
- *Subgrouping*—to have learners practice the application of new learning in small groups
- *Brainstorming*—to have learners generate ideas related to a key point or questions they would like to have answered
- *Educational games*—to illustrate a concept covered in the lecture or to review key points

Instructional Conference

The instructional conference is nothing more than a lecture that is broken up with periods for questions and discussion. Like the lecture, it is intended for learners who have no background knowledge or experience in the subject. The trainer lectures in short segments (about ten to fifteen minutes). After each segment, the trainer provides an opportunity for the learners to ask questions. The trainer also asks questions about the material just covered. This method incorporates planned feedback and comprehension checks. The question-and-answer periods also serve to break up the monotony of listening to the same person speaking all the time. The trainer may also be able to generate some discussion during the breaks between lecture segments.

Such conferences also have limitations. The trainer must prepare effective questions ahead of time that stimulate learner interest; this can be difficult to do with introductory-level material. The trainer must also decide where the logical breaking points are for asking the questions and soliciting feedback.

Steps

- The trainer lectures for ten to fifteen minutes.
- The trainer offers learners the opportunity to ask questions or comment.
- The trainer asks questions related to the content of the lecture.
- Learners respond to the questions.
- The first four steps are repeated until the presentation is completed.
- The trainer summarizes and provides closing remarks.

Complementary Methods

- *Independent practice*—to have learners apply concepts taught in the lecture and to reinforce learning
- *Study assignment*—to provide more in-depth knowledge or a frame of reference for putting new concepts into context; can also enable the trainer to move on to an intermediate-level method by providing learners with sufficient background knowledge

Complementary Strategies

- *Subgrouping*—to have learners practice the application of new learning in small groups

- *Buzz session*—to have learners discuss an aspect of the subject in small groups
- *Brainstorming*—to have learners generate ideas related to the objective or questions they would like to have answered
- *Educational games*—to depict a concept discussed or to provide a review

A relevant technique is the effective use of questions. Refer to Chapter Six for specific guidelines.

Guided Practice

With this instructional method, the trainer guides the learners through a task by having them practice each step separately. The learners watch the trainer demonstrate the first step of a task and immediately practice that step. The trainer then demonstrates the second step of the task and the learners practice it. This step-by-step procedure continues until the entire task has been demonstrated and practiced. The trainer ensures that everyone is performing a given step correctly before moving on to the next.

Some subjects that lend themselves to the guided practice method include the use of computers and equipment, first aid tasks, physical fitness training, cooking, and completing standardized forms.

This method also has limitations. Because learners work individually, it can be resource intensive (depending on the type of equipment needed). For example, a computer-based task would require that each learner have his or her own computer. The method does not lend itself to large groups because the trainer could not check each learner's progress after each step of the task. Even in small groups, the trainer may need assistants to help check learner progress.

Steps

- The trainer explains and demonstrates how to perform the first step of the task.
- Each learner practices the first step of the task.

- The trainer ensures that each learner has performed the first step correctly. The trainer may ask check questions or move around the group to personally observe learner performance, and provides corrective feedback as necessary.
- The trainer continues guiding the learners step-by-step until the task is completed.

Complementary Methods

- *Lecture*—to provide knowledge relevant to performing the task
- *Instructional conference*—to provide knowledge relevant to performing the task
- *Demonstration*—to allow learners to observe the correct way to perform the task before they practice it along with the trainer
- *Tutorial*—to provide specific corrective feedback for learners who require assistance
- *Independent practice*—to reinforce the task learned through repetition

Complementary Strategies

- *Subgrouping*—to have learners practice in small groups and assist each other via peer instruction

A relevant technique is for the trainer to be certain that all learners are performing a given step correctly before moving on to the next one. This may mean moving around the classroom and assisting learners on an individual basis.

Intermediate-Level Instructional Methods

Use these five methods when learners have prior experience related to the subject, or in introductory-level courses after learners have acquired some knowledge through reading and classes.

Developmental Conference

A developmental conference is a discussion where participants learn from one another's experiences related to the subject at hand. Participants extend their practical knowledge through their comments to one another as well as by learning the experiences of others, comparing ideas and opinions, and sharing information. Learners converse with each other and with the trainer. The trainer acts as a facilitator to allow everyone the opportunity to participate.

This method has its limitations. The trainer must be able to facilitate a group discussion and keep it focused on the topic. Participants may clash with differing opinions, discuss irrelevant points, or ramble on long after a point has been made. The use of time becomes critical with this method. Learners must have had experiences related to the topic in order to have a productive discussion. The method should be limited to small classes of fifteen or fewer learners.

Steps

- The trainer asks thought-provoking questions related to the topic.
- Learners answer the questions.
- The trainer solicits feedback from other learners, such as comments, opinions, and experiences to share.
- The trainer contributes ideas to the discussion only if it is apparent that the learners are not going to address them.
- The trainer raises key questions related to the topic as necessary until the discussion is finished.

Note: ideally, the learners will become engaged in spontaneous discussion after the trainer raises a few open-ended questions to get things started. When this occurs, the trainer withdraws from the discussion. The trainer will mainly be a facilitator at this point.

Complementary Methods

- *Role play*—to practice interpersonal skills if these are related to the topic
- *Case study*—to practice problem solving and decision making
- *Incident process*—to practice analytical skills needed to solve a problem
- *In-basket exercise*—to practice prioritizing assignments and making decisions

Complementary Strategies

- *Critical incident*—to learn from one another's past experiences
- *Buzz session*—to further discuss specific aspects of the topic in small groups of five or six
- *Brainstorming*—to generate alternative ideas, solutions to problems, or procedures

Relevant Techniques

- The questions the trainer poses must be open-ended in nature.
- The group should be seated in a circle or horseshoe so that everyone can see each other.
- The trainer must avoid talking too much so as not to stifle learner participation.
- The sequence in which key points are covered is not critical. Ideas should be addressed at the time they are brought up and not postponed until later in the discussion.
- Ideas may be recorded on newsprint for the group. If this technique is used, record *all* ideas, not just those of selected learners.

Peer Coaching

In this method, learners are divided into pairs to practice a task. They take turns coaching and practicing the task. The learner in the role of coach gives feedback to the learner practicing the task. The trainer observes the learners as they practice and provides feedback as necessary. This method can be used for both hands-on tasks such as applying a tourniquet and tasks that require interpersonal skills such as interviewing for a job. Peer coaching can also be used to capitalize on a given learner's expertise. When used in this way, the roles of coaching and practicing are not reversed.

The method is limited, however, in that learners must be able to distinguish correct procedures from incorrect ones so they can provide useful feedback to one another.

Steps

- The trainer describes how the method is used.
- Learners select a partner.
- The peer coach observes the learner perform the task.
- The peer coach gives feedback to the learner.
- The trainer monitors the pairs as they practice and may make suggestions as appropriate.
- Learners reverse roles.
- If appropriate, the learners practice the task or a portion of it again, incorporating feedback received from the peer coach.

Complementary Methods

- *Lecture*—to provide knowledge relevant to performing the task
- *Instructional conference*—to provide knowledge relevant to performing the task
- *Demonstration*—to allow learners to observe the correct way to perform the task
- *Role play*—to practice interpersonal skills that are incorporated into the task
- *Tutorial*—to provide individualized assistance as necessary

A relevant technique is for the trainer to move about the room and observe the learners during these practice sessions and provide additional assistance as necessary.

Independent Practice

With this method, learners practice a task individually. The type of task being taught determines how much independent practice is necessary. Independent practice may take the form of written exercises that require learners to apply what they have learned in a new context; the hands-on practice of a skill, such as typing, playing music, or cooking; or verbal practice, such as rehearsing a speech or practicing the pronunciation of words for a foreign language class.

But the method has limitations in that individual learners may vary in how much time they need to practice the task; some may finish long before others. Tasks that are complex may require constant trainer supervision rather than an occasional check. Assistant trainers may be needed to supervise the practice.

Steps

- Learners receive instruction on how to complete the task.
- The trainer provides the learners with any necessary equipment or materials to practice the task.
- The learners practice the task independently.
- The trainer assists each learner as needed on an individual basis.

Complementary Methods

- *Lecture*—to provide knowledge relevant to performing the task
- *Instructional conference*—to provide knowledge relevant to performing the task
- *Tutorial*—to provide individualized assistance to learners as necessary
- *Peer coaching*—to provide additional practice and feedback

Relevant Techniques

- Avoid lengthy practice sessions. Practicing one hour a day for five consecutive days is more effective than practicing for five hours on one day. If the task requires more than one hour to complete, ensure that the learners take a break about every fifty minutes.
- Give specific feedback when learners make errors. Tell the learner exactly what to do differently to correct the error.

Team Practice

With team practice, learners practice a *collective* task—one that requires a group of people to accomplish. Some examples of collective tasks are team sports, a band concert, a television or theater production, or planning a major political campaign. Not everyone in the group has the same assignment. For example, members of a baseball team play different roles: pitcher, catcher, and others. Team practice is necessary to ensure that the group is coordinated when the collective task is performed.

The method has limitations, however, as learners may be required to master more than one assignment within a collective task. For example, a journalism assignment might require learning several different aspects of publishing a newspaper. Time constraints may prevent everyone from practicing each function they are responsible for learning.

Steps

- Learners are formed into teams and given a project to complete.
- Each team member is responsible for his or her particular assignment but must also coordinate and cooperate with the other members of the team.
- When the teams have completed the project, they assess their performance. The members discuss how they made decisions, how they coordinated with one another, and what they learned from the experience. The trainer may add additional observations.

Complementary Methods

- *Lecture*—to provide knowledge relevant to the team's project
- *Instructional conference*—to provide knowledge relevant to the team's project
- *Demonstration*—to show how specific skills included as part of the team project are performed
- *Role play*—to improve interpersonal skills necessary to achieve consensus
- *Independent practice*—if individual assignments within the overall team project are complicated, they need to be practiced alone. For example, actors rehearse their lines alone before they rehearse with other cast members.
- *Peer coaching*—to practice individual assignments that are part of the team project

If the learning objective of the team's assignment emphasizes decision making or problem-solving skills, a relevant technique is to let the team work independently. Be available as a resource, but stay in the background.

Role Play

In a role play, learners act out real-world situations they are likely to encounter. A scenario is presented with roles to be played. Selected learners act the part of their assigned roles. The other learners observe. After the role play, the learners discuss their reactions to what happened. Role plays are used to increase awareness of interpersonal problems and to practice new behaviors for handling situations.

Role plays can be set up two ways: the players can attempt to speak, think, and behave like someone else, or they can play themselves in a given scenario. Acting like someone else—for example, playing an irate customer—teaches learners to identify with other people and their problems and to appreciate different perspectives. Playing oneself can help a person prepare for situations that he or she is likely to encounter—for example, resolving the conflict with the irate customer.

Role plays can be conducted in pairs, small groups, or in front of a large group. Learners may suggest situations they expect to encounter and experiment with different behaviors for handling them. The same scene can be replayed to demonstrate alternative approaches.

The method nevertheless has limitations. Learners must be prepared for the roles they play. For example, if the subject were resolving customer complaints, the learners would first be taught company policy and recommended techniques for diffusing hostility. Also, some learners may feel uncomfortable with this method. Role-play situations that are likely to evoke intense emotions are not appropriate for training. Intense role plays can be detrimental and are best reserved for use by those who have the required specialized training.

Steps

- The trainer presents the role-play scenario.

- The trainer asks for volunteers to play the roles.
- The trainer may request the observers to note specific items—behaviors, reactions, and the like.
- The role players act out the scenario.
- The trainer cuts off the role play at an appropriate point.
- The group analyzes the role play.

Complementary Methods

- *Lecture*—to provide knowledge necessary for learners to assume their roles
- *Instructional conference*—to provide knowledge necessary for learners to assume their roles
- *Demonstration*—to depict an alternative approach; for example, demonstrating a technique for calming an angry customer different from the one used during the role play
- *Case study*—to relate the role play to decision making
- *Peer coaching*—to practice communications or human-relations skills critical to dealing with difficult people or situations

A relevant technique here is to stop the role play at a high point—usually within ten minutes. Role plays can lose their effect if allowed to continue too long. Use probing questions during the analysis of the role play so that learners may arrive at their own insights. These work well: What happened? How well did you predict the reactions of others? How else might you have approached this situation? What might have been a more effective approach? What did you learn from this?

Advanced-Level Instructional Methods

Use these three methods to teach higher-order thinking skills such as analysis, decision making, and problem solving. Learners should already have learned both the principles and theory of the subject matter. Ideally, learners will also have some prior field experience.

Case Study

Using a case study means providing a realistic situation to the group for analysis. Learners may also be assigned independent research. Ultimately, the learners must decide how to resolve the problem or problems presented in the case. A successful resolution requires that they separate the significant facts from the insignificant ones. They must also draw conclusions from the significant facts and make decisions based on those conclusions. Learners must connect principles they have learned to the case. The object is for the learners to select the best alternative. This method develops analytical skills and ties theory to practice.

Case studies have limitations in that they are time-consuming to write because they require multiple higher-level learning objectives and a great deal of background information for the learners to research. They are often developed collaboratively among trainers. The learners must meet independently in their respective small groups to work on the case. Sufficient time must be allotted for each group to present its analysis and for discussion by the entire group. The situation is described in great detail. Learners are often given supplementary reading materials related to the issues involved, such as copies of policy memoranda, personnel handbooks, meeting minutes, and the like.

Note: short case studies that are not very complicated can be used to have learners apply concepts they have learned in a course. These mini-case studies do not require extensive background on the part of the learners and can be used to teach a variety of subjects.

Steps

- The trainer presents the case (usually in written form) and provides any supplementary information.
- The trainer assigns any relevant reading or research.
- The trainer highlights key aspects of the case and explains the requirements for the assignment.

- The learners meet in small groups to discuss the case and prepare a recommended solution.
- Each group of learners presents its analysis and proposed solution.
- All learners discuss each group's proposed solution.
- The trainer summarizes the findings and assesses the various proposed solutions.

Complementary Methods

- *Developmental conference*—to examine key issues and critical assumptions
- *Role play*—to underscore the effect of subjective perceptions and interpersonal communications
- *Study assignment*—to allow groups in-class time to work on the case or conduct independent research

A relevant technique for this method is to have learners work in small groups, enabling them to manage larger and more complex cases to develop their solutions. A group size of four learners is optimal.

Incident Process

The incident process is a method used to teach decision making with an emphasis on asking the right questions. Learners are given a short synopsis of an incident that actually occurred (hence the name *incident process*). They must decide how to resolve the problems presented in the incident. The synopsis deliberately omits critical information; not all of the facts are provided. The objective is to obtain all of the necessary information via fact-finding questions.

The trainer knows the history of the incident. The learners are given an allotted amount of time to ask questions about the incident. The trainer only answers the specific questions asked and does not volunteer any additional information. After the time period has expired, the learners must decide what course of action to take. All of the recommendations are discussed. Finally, the trainer reveals the decision that was actually made. A class discussion follows in which learners analyze their decision-making process.

A limitation is that the trainer must be able to evaluate the alternative solutions recommended. Learners may propose solutions that are workable but differ from the solution that was actually used. The trainer must be able to envision the probable outcome of each recommendation.

Steps

- The trainer provides directions for the incident process method (these can be written).
- The trainer gives each learner a brief written description of the incident.
- Learners ask questions to obtain the information they believe they need.
- The trainer answers the learners' questions during the allotted period. Note: fifteen minutes is usually long enough.
- The learners draft a solution. Note: this is usually done in small groups. Allow twenty to thirty minutes.
- Each group presents its recommended solution.
- The class discusses each recommended solution.
- The trainer reveals what really happened when the incident occurred and how it was resolved. Any information the learners did not request that was critical to the resolution is given at this point.
- The learners assess their decision-making process.

Complementary Methods

- *Developmental conference*—to discuss proposed solutions
- *Role play*—to consider the influence of subjective factors such as perception and personal styles of communication
- *Study assignment*—to research information relevant to the incident
- *Case study*—to practice separating essential facts from nonessential facts and to analyze what type of information decision makers need

Relevant Techniques

- Have the learners work in small groups to devise solutions. A group size of four learners is optimal.

- Check with each group after about fifteen minutes to see if you need to adjust the time they need to agree upon a solution.

In-Basket Exercise

In an in-basket exercise, each learner receives a set of materials that simulate what an employee in a given position, a manager for example, might expect to find in the in-basket on a typical work day. Typical items relate to delegating work assignments, planning employee work schedules, scheduling meetings, responding to various requests, and dealing with complaints. The folder often also contains a brief job description, an organization chart, a list of subordinates, and other pertinent information. The learners must respond to each item within a given time period. They write their response to each item on a separate sheet of paper. The responses are written in the form of notes, memos, letters, instructions to subordinates, meeting agendas—just as they would be written on the job. The folder often deliberately contains more items than can possibly be completed. This is done to see if the learners will prioritize items and to simulate time pressures typical of the position.

A limitation to this is that writing effective in-basket exercises often requires the work of more than one person. Also, it is very time-consuming to evaluate each learner's work.

Steps

- The trainer explains how to complete the in-basket exercise and informs the learners of the time limit.
- The trainer distributes a folder to each learner.
- Learners respond to as many items as possible during the allotted time.
- The learners discuss each item to include the pros and cons of each proposed solution.
- If necessary, the trainer identifies the preferred solution and explains the reasons for selecting it. Note: hopefully the learners will identify the preferred solution themselves during the discussion.

- The trainer determines if anyone prioritized items. If not, the trainer directs the learners' attention to the critical items placed in the back of the folder.
- Learners discuss their reactions to the exercise.
- The key points are summarized. Note: either the trainer or one of the learners can provide the summary.

Complementary Methods

- *Team practice*—an in-basket can be one of the assignments used in a project assigned as part of the team practice method
- *Study assignment*—can precede the in-basket exercise to review background information that will be needed to complete the exercise
- *Role play*—can be used to dramatize how people might react to the decisions made during the in-basket exercise
- *Incident process*—can be used to emphasize the importance of obtaining complete and relevant information prior to making a decision

Relevant Techniques

- Make sure the directions for completing the in-basket are specific, as this method is new to many people. It's helpful to put them in writing.
- Be sure the discussion of the in-basket exercise includes the concept of prioritizing one's work.
- Allow learners an opportunity to discuss the rationale they used to make their decisions before stating the preferred solution.

Instructional Methods for All Levels

The four methods that follow are not contingent on the amount of background learners have in the subject.

Demonstration

The demonstration is a "show and tell" method. Learners observe the task being performed so they can see what it looks like when it is done correctly. The trainer explains the steps as they are performed. The trainer may conduct the demonstration or it may be presented via video-tape. Besides hands-on tasks, demonstrations may be used to teach interpersonal skills such as interviewing or counseling.

However, because all learners must be able to easily see a hands-on demonstration, class size may be limited. Extra time may need to be scheduled to allow for setup and teardown of equipment.

Steps

- Trainer provides background information to include the following:
  A "talk-through" of the basic steps
  Any tips or helpful hints to make the task easier, such as advising beginning drivers to always watch what is happening a block ahead
  Common mistakes beginners might make, such as cautioning beginning typists not to look at the keys
  Any safety precautions
  The standard learners should be able to achieve—for example, typing at least thirty-five words per minute with no more than five errors by the end of the course
- The trainer demonstrates the task or shows videotape of task.
- Learners practice the task as the trainer observes them and gives feedback.
- Once the trainer is assured that learners are performing the steps of the task correctly, learners practice independently.

Complementary Methods

- *Lecture*—to provide supplemental information
- *Instructional conference*—to provide supplemental information
- *Developmental conference*—to discuss tasks that require interpersonal skills
- *Role play*—to practice portions of a task requiring strong communications skills, such as answering a difficult question during a job interview
- *Guided practice*—to practice at a group pace before practicing individually
- *Independent practice*—to improve one's performance until the standard has been met or exceeded

Relevant Techniques

- Give learners immediate feedback on their progress. Walk around the room and comment on each learner's performance. If a learner is performing the steps correctly, a simple "that's right!" or "good!" will reinforce the progress. If a learner is performing the steps incorrectly, demonstrate specifically how to correct the error.
- Avoid practice sessions that are too lengthy. It is better to practice one hour a day for five consecutive days than to practice for five hours on one day. This way learners avoid fatigue. Learners are also less likely to forget what they have learned if they must use it on a frequent basis.
- Be sure all learners can easily see the task being demonstrated.
- For tasks that consist of several steps performed in a set sequence (such as CPR), give learners a handout that lists the steps in the order in which they are performed.
- Demonstrate one step of a task at a time, carefully explaining each step as you demonstrate it.

Tutorial

A tutorial simply means working with learners individually. Tutoring requires adapting one of the methods described in this chapter for use on a one-to-one basis. Tutoring is often linked with remedial learning but its use is much broader than that. Many skills cannot be effectively taught unless learners get a certain amount of individual assistance from the trainer. Some examples of skills that require tutoring to learn are individual sports, playing a musical instrument, speaking a foreign language, driving a car, and administering the Heimlich maneuver. Tutoring is also a common method used with learners who have been assigned individual projects, such as writing a computer program. The trainer schedules individual conferences to assist with any problems and give feedback about any portions of the project already completed.

Tutoring is extremely resource-intensive. It can only be used when time is available to meet individually with learners. Even then, it may not be possible unless assistant trainers are available to identify the learning problem and correct it.

Steps

- The trainer assigns a project to be completed or identifies a learner having difficulty.
- The trainer meets with the learner to assess the progress of the project or the nature of the learner's difficulty.
- The trainer assists the learner using a method appropriate for the learning objective.
- The trainer may act in a consultative role and suggest various alternative approaches.
- In remedial training, the trainer may coach the learner step-by-step through the task.

Complementary Methods

> *Note:* these will depend upon the method used in the tutorial.

- *Lecture*—to provide information relevant to the assigned project
- *Instructional conference*—to provide information relevant to the assigned project
- *Demonstration*—to reteach correct performance to learners experiencing difficulty with a task
- *Independent practice*—to provide additional practice as necessary

A relevant technique for this method is to be sure to plan something for the rest of the class to do if you assist learners on an individual basis during the regular class meeting time.

Programmed Instruction

Programmed instruction is a self-paced method in which the instruction is presented via a book or a computer program. Information is presented in small segments. After each segment, the learner is required to answer questions or perform a task. The "program" lets the learner know immediately if the question was answered correctly (or the task performed correctly). Programmed instruction is interactive, as the learners must continuously respond to what the program prompts them to do.

Learners must master each segment of information before the program will allow them to progress to the next level of difficulty. If a learner answers a question incorrectly, the program may review information previously presented and then ask the question again. Normally a resource person is available to assist learners who cannot get beyond a given point in the program. Programs that assign the learners tasks—for example, to create a sales chart using information provided in the lesson—definitely require that the trainer be available to assist students who experience difficulty.

Note: programmed instruction must be developed by professionals who have been specifically trained. However, there are a number of programmed instruction materials that have already been developed and are available for purchase. For example, several computer software packages come with tutorial programs that allow users to teach themselves how to operate the program.

This method has several limitations. Programmed instruction is very expensive to have developed. Those programs that are presented via computer require that each learner have a computer available to use. Furthermore, because programmed instruction is self-paced, learners will finish at different times; this can create scheduling problems.

Steps

- The trainer describes the program.
- The trainer explains administrative procedures, such as how much time is allotted, where the trainer will be if anyone needs help, and the like.

- The trainer directs learners to the instructions (which will be incorporated into the program itself).
- Learners complete the program (or an assigned portion of it) at their own pace.
- Learners may be required to produce a product either intermittently or at the end of the program.
- The trainer assists individual learners as needed.

Complementary Methods

- *Lecture*—to explain related concepts
- *Instructional conference*—to explain related concepts
- *Independent practice*—to provide additional practice as needed
- *Demonstration*—to clarify how to perform a task or steps of a task if learners are confused by the programmed instruction's lesson

Relevant Techniques

- Allow enough time for *all* learners to be able to complete the lesson. Some tasks vary widely in this regard. It is possible that some learners will take as much as three times longer than others to work through the same lesson.
- Arrange for flexible scheduling to allow those who finish early to either be able to leave early or go on to something else.

Teaching Strategies: Supplements to Methods

A teaching strategy is a specific procedure used to *supplement* a method. Strategies are always used along with methods; they cannot substitute for methods. As a general rule, they are only used for short periods of time. Use strategies to add interest to a method, increase the level of learner participation, or capitalize on the collective knowledge of the group. This section describes six basic teaching strategies.

Subgrouping

In subgrouping, learners work in small groups of usually four to six people. Each group has an assignment to complete, such as to analyze a brief case study. If a goal is to generate many different ideas or perspectives regarding a problem, then each subgroup should be working on the same problem. Alternatively, each group may work on different aspects of a problem or be assigned different tasks to complete related to the learning objective. At the end of an allotted time period, each group presents its findings to the class as a whole. Subgrouping is often used to create opportunities for participation in large groups. Another benefit of subgrouping is that learners are apt to learn from each other; questions may be clarified that might not have been asked in front of a large group. Learners also get a chance to socialize a little which makes for a more relaxed atmosphere overall.

A limitation of subgrouping is that sometimes the participation is unbalanced—some learners may not contribute while others may contribute too much.

Tips for Use

- Explain the assignment and inform the group of the timelines—that is, how much time they will have to work and how much time each group will have to report its findings. If the directions are lengthy, put them in writing.
- Remind the learners that each subgroup will report its findings to the entire group. They may wish to make notes as they work.
- Check with the groups periodically—there will probably be questions after learners begin working.

Note: if you use this strategy often, vary the composition of the groups. This allows learners in a large class to meet more people and allows for exposure to a variety of perspectives.

Buzz Session

In a buzz session, the learners form small groups of between four and six people for the purpose of discussing a topic. In formal courses that include tests, buzz groups may be used to identify areas the learners would like reviewed. Unlike the subgroup, the learners are not expected to complete an assignment or resolve a problem. The idea is to stimulate thought. Therefore, the buzz session is relatively short—ten minutes is usually sufficient. The trainer leads a discussion of the whole class after the buzz session is finished.

A drawback to buzz sessions is that participation may be unbalanced, with some learners not contributing to the discussion and others contributing too much.

Tips for Use

- Explain the purpose for the buzz session.
- If using this strategy frequently, vary the composition of the groups. This allows learners in a large class to meet more people and allows for exposure to a variety of perspectives.

Brainstorming

For brainstorming, learners form small groups of between four and six people for the purpose of generating as many ideas as possible regarding an assigned topic. This is done in two phases. In phase one, the group generates ideas quickly *without discussing them*. A person from each group records all of the ideas suggested, even duplicates. (Duplicates can be indicated with checkmarks or initials.) Ideas are recorded on an easel board for all to see. In phase two, the group discusses and evaluates the ideas. Some ideas may be eliminated after this. The product of phase two will be a list of what the group believes to be the best ideas. Usually five to ten minutes is allowed for generating ideas in phase one. Phase two lasts for between ten and fifteen minutes. The class is reconvened as a whole and each group presents its ideas.

Tips for Use

- Emphasize that the brainstorming will be conducted in two phases: listing ideas and evaluating them. In the first phase no comments are allowed; all ideas are simply recorded (even if the same idea is repeated). The concept is to keep the flow of ideas coming without interruption. In phase one, the goal is quantity—the more ideas the better.
- If necessary, remind learners of the rules: they are not to evaluate during phase one, and *all* ideas must be listed.
- During each phase, inform the students when half of the time has elapsed.

Panel Discussion

For a panel discussion, a group of three to six learners each take turns presenting a brief (five- to ten-minute) talk related to a discussion topic. Individual panelists may speak about specific portions of the overall topic (for example, discussing a country with different panelists addressing its geography, economics, politics, and culture) or may represent a different point of view related to an issue (for example, different political perspectives). After all have finished presenting, the panelists answer questions from the class. Panelists can also debate issues among themselves; if so, a moderator is needed to allow equal time for all points of view.

A limitation: as the panelists are in effect teaching a part of the class, the trainer must be sure that they are fully prepared.

Tips for Use

- The trainer may need to meet with panelists individually to assist them in preparing their presentations.
- Wait until all panelists have presented before opening up the question-and-answer session. This is especially important if the panelists are presenting different points of view. Otherwise you may run out of time before all panelists have had a chance to present.

Critical Incident

With the critical incident strategy, learners share experiences they have had that relate to the course. It might be a decision once made and the outcome of that decision. The critical incident itself could be either a positive or negative experience. However, it should be an incident that was perceived as a significant learning experience.

But to use this strategy, learners must have real-world experience related to the course content. The strategy usually isn't suited for introductory-level courses. Also, it is time-consuming and cannot be used in large classes unless you limit the number of learners who relate a critical incident.

Tips for Use

- Allow learners enough time to reflect about a critical incident.
- Not everyone will be able to quickly respond to a request such as, "In your experience as a customer service representative, describe an incident that happened from which you learned a great deal." Consider asking the learners to identify a critical incident a day or two before the class discussion.

Educational Games

Educational games may take the format of a popular board game or a television game, or may have a unique design. Games can be as simple as recalling information or as elaborate as simulated operations of a large corporation.

Games do not need to be elaborate. Many well-known games can easily be adapted for classroom use by changing the type of knowledge they require to be successful. One popular format is the jigsaw puzzle design: individual learners are given "pieces" to put together to complete a "picture." The picture may or may not be visual. For example, learners may have been given different facts needed to solve a problem. In this instance the game would demonstrate the importance of sharing information in addition to teaching problem-solving skills.

Note: commercially produced educational games exist in a number of different content areas that include team building, diversity training, general management, and interpersonal communications.

Avoid complex games unless you have advanced-level learners and a great deal of time to spend on the game.

Tips for Use

- Consider specifically what the game should accomplish. Do you want to illustrate a concept? Review facts? Encourage creativity? Determine the purpose of the game before you start developing it.
- Make sure you provide clear directions. Unless the directions are extremely simple, put them in writing.

◆ ◆ ◆

Selecting instructional methods (and their related strategies and techniques) is one of the most important decisions you will make when planning a training workshop. This will affect several dimensions of the training: learner interest and participation, the amount of time needed to present a given topic, and possibly whether or not the learning objectives are met. You must always consider the subject of the training, class size, resources, and the background of the learners when deciding which methods to use. A mismatch with any of these factors can cause any method to be ineffective. One of the most important principles of training is to get people actively involved. Remember: The treasure of learning is in the joy of the discovery!

PLANNING SHEET 3: METHODS AND STRATEGIES

Considerations

SUBJECT

_____

_____

_____

CLASS SIZE

_____

_____

RESOURCES

_____

_____

Time

_____

_____

Space

_____

_____

Other

_____

_____

_____

Learners' Background

_____

_____

POSSIBLE METHODS

_____

_____

_____

_____

_____

INSTRUCTIONAL TECHNIQUES

_____

_____

_____

_____

POSSIBLE STRATEGIES

_____

_____

_____

_____

NOTES

_____

_____

_____

_____

CHAPTER FOUR

CHOOSING AND USING TRAINING AIDS

The Peacock and the Crane

A boastful Peacock met a Crane one day and tried to impress him with his colorful tail. As he spread his tail to reveal all its beautiful colors, he said, "I dare you to compare even one of your dull feathers with any of mine! I have more colors than the most glorious rainbow! How can your feathers begin to compare with mine?" At that moment the Crane spread his wings and flew up into the sky. "Follow me if you can," he said. But the Peacock was destined to remain with the barnyard birds and could only watch in awe as the Crane soared higher and higher into the horizon. The useful is of much more importance and value than the ornamental.

Keep in mind when choosing training aids that the useful is indeed of much more importance and value than the ornamental. Training aids include any materials or equipment used to support a training session. Handouts, flip charts, 35mm slides, overhead transparencies, videotapes, and computers are examples of commonly used training aids. They assist learning by involving one or more of the senses (sight, sound, touch, smell, or taste) and can be as simple as a drawing or as complex as a flight simulator used to train airplane pilots.

Training aids are used for a variety of reasons:

- To practice the learning objective for hands-on tasks, such as using a mannequin to learn CPR or a computer to create a document
- To emphasize a key point
- To summarize and review
- To give a visual representation of a concept, such as a graph or an organizational chart
- To demonstrate a concept in a concrete way, such as showing a videotape of an effective method of appeasing an irate customer
- To make a point in a different way—for example, showing a transparency of a humorous cartoon that underscores the importance of backing up one's computer files to a disk
- To simplify a point

- To focus attention on a specific area, such as pointing out a particular area on a transparency of a map
- To add variety and interest

The Lioness and the Vixen

A Lioness and a Vixen were discussing the traits of their children. Both were well pleased with their offspring. The Vixen, in an attempt to prove that she was indeed more fortunate than the Lioness, said, "My litter of cubs is an absolute joy to behold, but I see that you only have one." "It's true

I only have one," retorted the Lioness, "but that one's a lion." The value is in the worth, not in the number.

The principle of quality over quantity cannot be overemphasized regarding the use of training aids. As the name implies, training aids are an aid to, not a substitute for, instruction. Avoid overusing training aids or they will lose their effect. If virtually every point you make is written on an overhead transparency, the learners will have a hard time distinguishing the key points from the supporting points. Too many "gee-whiz" effects from training aids can shift the learners' focus from the idea under consideration to the technology being used to stress it.

Let's look at different types of training aids.

Handouts

Handouts are pages of printed material that you give to the learners. They can be extracts from longer works, bibliographies for future reading, directions for completing a task, sample forms, summaries of topics, or outlines for note-taking. Use handouts to provide information that is too detailed or complex to use on a flip chart or transparency.

Tips for Use

- Don't violate copyright law. With the convenience of copying machines, it can be tempting to copy pages from books or other sources for use as handouts. But copyrighted material requires prior written permission to reproduce, distribute, or display. A *few* publishers will allow one-time-only use of a portion of the work for teaching purposes. Always check each publisher's copyright policy before using copyrighted material.
- Make sure you have enough copies for everyone.
- Distribute handouts at the time you want the learners to refer to them. If you give them out ahead of time, people will start reading them. An exception to this rule is if you would lose too much time by pass-

ing them out during the instruction. For example, if you have a large group of people and several different handouts, you could easily lose fifteen minutes by distributing the handouts piecemeal.

- If the handout contains several pages, number them consecutively for easy reference.

Chalkboards or Whiteboards

Chalkboards and whiteboards serve the same purpose: they can be used to list key points and to diagram and sketch. On both, new ideas and information can easily be added later. The more modern whiteboard eliminates chalk dust and can also be used as an overhead projection screen.

Tips for Use

- Print letters (don't use cursive writing) at least two inches high for good visibility.
- On chalkboards, use only white chalk. On whiteboards, use dark-colored markers (although available in many colors, only the dark colors are easily read from the back of the room). Red is especially difficult to read from a distance on whiteboards.
- Don't talk to the board. Write first, then look at the learners when speaking to them.
- If using a chalkboard, don't squeak the chalk! You can avoid this by holding the chalk at an angle to the board, using downward strokes, and not pressing too hard.
- Do not clean a whiteboard with water. Use only a dry towel or eraser to remove what you have written. These boards can only be cleaned with a specially formulated product or they will be damaged.
- Erase the material on the board once it no longer applies to the topic under discussion.

Flip Charts

Similar to the chalkboard, the flip chart allows for a permanent record of what you write. Flip charts are best reserved for use in small groups because not everyone in a large group would be able to read one easily. They are often used in conjunction with small-group discussions. Someone from the group records the key ideas as they are developed. A common practice is to tear off completed pages and tape them to the wall of the classroom. The group can then refer to all the ideas that were recorded. Flip charts can also be prepared in advance to present diagrams, charts, or graphs. In this case, the pages are not detached so that the trainer can reuse them with future classes.

Tips for Use

- Use only dark-colored markers.
- If you are acting as a recorder for the key points of a group discussion, write down all ideas. Do not edit someone's comment without asking the person if what you have written adequately captures the idea.
- Print (once again, no cursive) letters at least one inch high.

Overhead Transparencies

Probably the most commonly used training aid, transparencies are inexpensive and versatile. They can be as simple as writing on an acetate sheet with an audiovisual marker or as elaborate as a color photograph. You can make a transparency from anything that you can photocopy (but keep in mind that not all copiers can produce color transparencies). Computer graphics programs can also be used to create masters. They have options for bullet-type slides, charts, and graphics. You can even use a typewriter to create a master for a transparency with lines of text (as long as you later enlarge the text when you photocopy it and then use the photocopy as the master).

Design Guidelines for Transparencies

- Limit text to six lines, six words per line. Never make a transparency from an entire page of text. If you have wordy material, use a handout instead.
- Keep transparencies simple—eliminate unnecessary words or figures.
- Don't divide sections with lines. Use space instead.
- Use a horizontal format; words should read from left to right, not up or down.
- Use a horizontal (landscape) layout for transparencies. Overhead projectors are designed for transparencies to be placed on them horizontally. With 8½-by-11-inch paper, this layout means that the master is 11 inches across and 8½ inches deep.
- Allow for borders around each side of the transparency. The material must fit within a 7⅜-inch-by-9⅜-inch projection area in order to be displayed.
- Remember that copyright law also applies to transparencies. Some publishers may allow one for educational purposes. Always check each publisher's copyright policy before using copyrighted material.

Producing Your Own Transparencies

Transparencies are made either by using an infrared transparency maker or by using a copy machine that accepts transparency film loaded into the paper tray. As infrared transparency makers are not typically found in offices, you probably will use a copy machine. The first step to producing transparencies is to prepare the master.

If using a typewriter to create a transparency master:

- Use large type and set the typewriter for 10 pitch (pica).
- Allow ample space between lines.

- Make a copy of the master using the enlargement feature on the copier to enlarge the text as much as possible while still allowing it to fit within the projection area.

If using a computer graphics program to create a transparency master:

- Choose a block style letter at least one-quarter-inch high.
- Print the master in letter quality, not draft quality.

If using a photocopy as a transparency master, be sure you have a clean copy. Any stray marks or specks will transfer onto the transparency film.

Consider whether you need to enlarge an item. For example, if you want transparencies of a form, consider breaking it into sections and enlarging each section for better visibility. This also gives you the option of writing on it with an audiovisual marker to demonstrate how it's completed. Note: transparencies used to display forms are an exception to the rule of limiting text to six lines.

Once you have your masters prepared, you are ready to produce the actual transparencies using a copy machine:

1. Make a copy of each master.
2. Obtain the transparency film compatible with the copy machine you are using. This usually has a white strip on one edge.
3. Obtain cardboard mounting frames designed for transparencies.
4. Place the transparency film into the paper supply tray of the copier.
5. Make a copy of the photocopy you made for each master.
6. Remove the transparencies from the product tray.
7. Remove the transparency film from the paper tray.
8. Using masking tape, tape the back of the transparency to the back of the mounting frame.

Note: if you do not have access to a copy machine that accepts transparency film, you can have transparencies produced at a photocopy business.

Guidelines for Using Transparencies

- Proofread each transparency before use. Make sure the information is accurate and free of spelling errors.
- Be familiar with the overhead projector you will be using. Projectors vary slightly from brand to brand. Know where the on-off switch or button is located, how to focus, and how to change the bulb if it burns out. Carry an extra bulb with you in your briefcase.
- Try the transparencies out in advance. Go to the classroom and test each one. Make sure each is visible from the back of the room and that the full transparency is projecting without part of it being cut off.
- Check the lighting of the room. Full-color transparencies may not project unless the light is dimmed. Determine if the light will need to be adjusted for any of your transparencies.
- Number each transparency according to the sequence in which it will be displayed. Be consistent with how you number them—for example, always in the right-hand corner of the border.
- Check each transparency as you project it to make sure it is positioned correctly.
- Read it. Read the text to yourself twice before removing the transparency.
- Reveal lines of text one at a time to keep attention focused on a given point. Place a blank sheet of paper *underneath* the transparency and pull down as you go. (If you place the paper on top, it may slide off.)
- Do not keep a transparency projected when it no longer relates to what is being discussed.
- Turn off the projector between transparencies or use a cardboard flap taped onto the projector to darken the screen between transparencies. Viewing blank illuminated screens between transparencies requires the learners' eyes to constantly adjust to changes in light.
- If using a pointer, hold it in the arm closest to the screen. Hint: a mechanical pencil placed on the projector or an arrow cut from colored acetate works well as a pointer you can use without having to walk over to the screen.

- Avoid talking to the screen. Hint: use the copies of the transparency masters. This way you have what the learners are seeing in front of you and you won't need to look at the screen.
- Watch where you stand. Do not block the screen with your body.

35mm Slides

Viewing color photography or graphics on 35mm slides is visually interesting. They have the advantage of bringing examples from the real world into the classroom. Today, people with a basic knowledge of photography can produce their own 35mm slides. Some computer systems offer the option of making a color slide from a computer screen. Also, commercially produced slide programs are available. Two disadvantages to choosing slides are that they are considerably expensive and that the room must be completely darkened to show them.

Here are some guidelines for using 35mm slides:

- Know how the particular slide projector you are using works.
- Consult the operator's manual to determine how to position and elevate the projector.
- Project the image so that it completely fills the screen but does not spill over onto the wall.
- Ensure you have loaded the slides in the correct sequence.
- Check that the slides are inserted correctly so they won't project upside down or backward.
- Go to the classroom ahead of time to set up the projector and run through all of the slides.

Videotapes

The popularity of the video cassette recorder has resulted in hundreds of commercially produced videotapes for training purposes. Videotapes are available in a wide range of training areas. They are usually expensive to purchase; however, training departments of organizations often order them and libraries continue to expand their videotape collections. Videotapes can be used in different ways. They can be stopped at given points for discussion purposes. They can be viewed in part or in their entirety. Selected segments can be shown more than once.

Here are some guidelines for using videotapes:

- *Always* preview a tape you intend to use ahead of time. You cannot determine if it is appropriate by simply reading the written material that accompanies it. You also need to determine that it is not damaged.
- Remember that copyright law applies to commercial television programs.
- Familiarize yourself with the equipment you are using.
- Cue the videotape ahead of time. Have the picture quality and volume adjusted for the class. If showing a particular segment, have the tape advanced to the starting point you selected.
- Position the TV monitor so that everyone can see. Note: you should have (at a minimum) a twenty-five-inch-diagonal monitor for a group of twenty or fewer.
- Seat learners at least seven feet away from the monitor. Use the screen's diagonal dimension as a guideline for how far away in feet someone can be seated from it; for example, if you have a twenty-five-inch-diagonal monitor then no one should be seated more than twenty-five feet away.
- Be aware of electrical cords. If necessary, caution people so they don't trip on them.
- Tell the learners what they are about to see. If there is anything in particular you want them to focus on, let them know.
- Discuss the videotape after the learners have viewed it. Solicit their reactions and what they perceive the key points to be.

Computers

With the increasing use of computers to produce transparency masters and 35mm slides, many portable models have additional features that are useful to trainers. For example, some have the capability of projecting directly from the computer screen onto the projection screen in the classroom. In this case, there is no need to produce transparencies. Other features include laser pointers and the ability to make the symbol that precedes a bullet of text flash to indicate that's the item under discussion. If you have this type of system available to you, you can save time and work by learning how to use it.

As in the case of videotapes, hundreds of commercially produced computer programs are available for training purposes. These range from simple tutorials contained on a floppy disk to elaborate interactive multimedia programs. These programs are developed to meet very specific training objectives and are self-paced in format.

◆ ◆ ◆

Training aids are useful tools that can serve many purposes. They can help you present an idea in a different format. You can use them to emphasize or review a key point. Students are more likely to remember material presented via a training aid because more than one sense of perception is involved, such as sight or touch as well as sound. If designed well, training aids can also add variety and interest to a presentation.

Training aids, like any tool, must be used correctly to be effective. An award-winning videotape relevant to your topic is of little value if most of the learners literally can't see it because it is being shown on a nineteen-inch monitor and they are seated thirty feet away. Remember that training aids are used to *support* instruction. Too many training aids can create an information overload for learners. There should be a reason why each training aid is being used.

PLANNING SHEET 4: TRAINING AIDS

Possible Training Aids

HANDOUTS

_____

_____

_____

_____

_____

_____

_____

_____

_____

_____

CHALKBOARD OR WHITEBOARD CONTENT

_____

_____

_____

_____

_____

_____

_____

_____

_____

_____

FLIP CHART USE

_____
_____
_____
_____
_____
_____
_____
_____
_____
_____
_____

OVERHEAD TRANSPARENCIES

_____
_____
_____
_____
_____
_____
_____
_____
_____
_____
_____
_____
_____

35mm SLIDES

_____

_____

_____

_____

_____

_____

_____

_____

VIDEOTAPES

_____

_____

_____

_____

_____

_____

_____

_____

COMPUTER SLIDE SHOW

_____

_____

_____

_____

_____

_____

NOTES

CHAPTER FIVE

MAKING EXPLANATIONS CLEAR

The Fox and the Cat

A Fox was telling a Cat about all the different tricks he had to escape from dogs. "I have more tricks up my sleeve than I can count," he said. "Tell me some of yours." The Cat, somewhat embarrassed, said, "There's only one way I know to escape dogs. I simply run up a tree."

Suddenly a pack of dogs came by. The Fox, despite all his fancy tricks, was so startled that he could not decide which one to use. He was easily caught by the dogs. The Cat instinctively ran up a tree and was quickly out of danger. You can count on the tried and true.

You can count on the tried and true in training too. When you think of trainers you have known, you probably remember some as being very effective and others as being very ineffective. Even those who are highly competent within the subject matter they teach do not always teach effectively. They can't understand why their learners are lost. Many cases of poor instruction can be traced to a violation of one or more of the guidelines listed in this chapter.

If you follow these guidelines, you will greatly increase the chances that the learners will reach the learning objectives. Use these guidelines in both planning and presenting training courses.

Identify and Emphasize Key Points

The average person speaks at a rate of 150 words per minute. This amounts to 9,000 words per hour. If you listened to 9,000 words on a topic that was new to you, how would you know what was critical and what was not? This is the dilemma faced by learners as they take notes. Unless the trainer does something to emphasize the key points, the learners may miss them.

What to Identify

You as the trainer must identify those points that need to be stressed. Determining which points are key is a matter of asking yourself some questions.

What Is Absolutely Essential to Meet the Learning Objective or Perform the Task Successfully? Some steps of a task may be much more critical than others. For example, a sales trainee may be learning different techniques to close a sale. However, if the trainee cannot establish rapport with a potential customer, there's a good chance the sale will be lost. Therefore, teaching the trainee to establish rapport is a concept that should be emphasized. A hospital laboratory technician may learn the steps for determining a white blood cell count. However, if the

technician did not know the normal range for the cell count, a report that should be immediately sent to the doctor could be dangerously delayed. Therefore, the ranges for normal and abnormal counts need to be stressed.

If you are teaching a task, consider which steps are *crucial* to successful completion of the task. When I once made some chocolate candy, I was disappointed with the results. I later learned from a friend that I let the chocolate get too hot when I was melting it. This *one* step of the task, melting the chocolate, affected the final product. This step was *critical* to a successful outcome.

When teaching an information-based subject, consider what concepts or ideas are essential to the overall learning objective.

What Is Difficult to Learn? If you are in the position of teaching the same subject on a continuing basis, you will develop a sense of what learners find difficult to grasp. Sometimes learners struggle with concepts that do not seem difficult to you. Also, if you test the learners you may see a pattern of error, such as several of them missing question three. This is a cue to you to emphasize the topic tested by question three the next time you teach the subject. Listen to the questions that learners ask. Were several about any one topic? If so, that topic needs to be emphasized. Try to remember when *you* learned the subject or task for the first time. What aspects seemed difficult at that time? What seemed difficult to you probably is difficult for your learners.

Are Safety Factors Involved in the Task? Always stress safety precautions *before* learners begin practicing the task. Also include any guidelines to prevent damage to equipment.

Are You Already Aware of Problems the Learners Have Experienced with the Task You're Training Them to Perform? You may have been hired to conduct training because of problems encountered on the job. For instance, perhaps a company converted to new computer software that now requires the use of a mouse instead of performing functions via keystrokes. The person who coordinated the training may have mentioned that the employees were having difficulty using the mouse.

As you already know this, mouse techniques should become a key point in the training.

What to Emphasize

Once you have identified the key points, you must decide how to emphasize them so that the learners are likely to remember them. Here are some ways to emphasize key points.

Spend Ample Time Discussing the Point. The amount of time spent teaching a concept should be proportionate to its importance. When important material is covered quickly, learners will not realize its importance. Conversely, avoid tangents on minor points.

Ask Check Questions That Correspond to the Key Points. Avoid check questions that relate to trivial points or low-level check questions that don't really measure understanding.

Use Visual Aids to Highlight Key Points. Here are several possibilities:

- List them on a chalkboard or easel board.
- Provide an outline for notetaking.
- Use an overhead projector.
- Summarize key points in a handout.
- Show a related videotape or clip from a videotape.
- Cue learners with phrases such as:
     This idea is really important because . . .
     This is the key to understanding . . .
     You will use this time and time again when you must . . .
     This is critical . . .
     If you don't remember anything else, remember this . . .
- Change your voice dynamics. State the main point in a louder tone or pause for emphasis.
- Relate an anecdote from your experience that illustrates the importance of the point you are making.

- Use humor. Perhaps you know a joke that underscores a point you want to make. Note: be sure jokes you use are relevant to the point or learners will remember the joke and not the point! Be sure any joke you tell is not going to offend anyone.

Important note: Avoid information overload! Limit the number of key points to no more than seven per hour of instruction. A common mistake new trainers make is not allowing enough time to thoroughly cover the key points. The result is a pace too fast for effective learning.

Use Examples

Examples are bridges that take the learners from a familiar idea or concept to one that is unfamiliar to them. Therefore, in order to be effective, learners must be familiar with the examples you use. Always consider the background of your learners when choosing an example. Examples of specific people or events may be before the time of a young class. Using an example of a particular senator to illustrate a leadership style will not work if the group isn't inclined to follow political news.

It's a good idea to plan examples ahead of time; they're not always easy to think of on the spot. Every key point should have at least one example to illustrate it.

Review What You Have Taught

Repetition is an essential ingredient in any training context. Do not assume that just because you made a statement that everyone will remember it. People forget new material easily. Also, not everyone will completely understand an idea the first time it is presented. As a trainer, you must be patient about repeating items previously explained. A review enables you to make the same point in a different way. Reviews do not have to be lengthy to be effective. They can be brief highlights of key points discussed. You can also use check questions as a form of review.

As a general rule, review after about each twenty minutes of instruction. When you stop to review, first ask if anyone has questions about what has been covered. The type of questions asked can be a cue for you to review specific concepts. This is especially true if several learners have questions about a particular area.

Organize Your Material

Part of planning a training session is determining the sequence in which to explain each topic. What will be discussed first, second, third, and so on? Sequencing affects how easy or difficult it is to follow the instruction. This is especially true when the learners have little or no background in the subject. The type of content you will be teaching is a guide for how to organize the material. More than one sequence design can be used during a training session if the topics covered are varied or if learners have background knowledge in some topics but not others.

Simple to Complex

Use this design when you teach material that gets progressively more difficult—that "snowballs." This sequence assumes that one subject or skill becomes a stepping stone to learning the next one. Begin with the basics and gradually progress to the more advanced areas. Remember to define terms that are new to the learners. Avoid confusing them with references to concepts that are still foreign to them. For example, to refer to terms like *batch files* and *macros* on the first day of a word processing course will only make anxious learners even more anxious. Be sure they have acquired the fundamental concepts before moving on to more challenging ones.

General to Specific

This sequence lends itself to subjects that are either highly detailed (such as tax preparation) or abstract in nature (such as leadership). To use this design, begin by providing an overview of the topic so that learners have a frame of reference for the more specific information that will come later. In teaching a tax preparation course, an overview might include the purpose of each schedule, the percentage of returns including a given schedule, and common problems or errors encountered. Each schedule should be discussed in *general* terms before learners are shown how to complete each *specific* item on it. In a workshop on leadership, it would be helpful to first discuss different leadership theories and styles before analyzing a case study to determine if XYZ Company has effective leadership.

Specific to General

Sometimes referred to as "discovery learning" or "inductive reasoning," this design is used to require learners to make inferences from specific data, for instance, analyzing why a machine isn't working properly or determining what motivates an employee described in a case study. This sequence is used only after learners have acquired sufficient background knowledge in the subject.

Concrete to Abstract

This sequence design is always used with at least one other design. The principle of moving from the concrete to the abstract is to ensure that learners can visualize whatever it is you are explaining. For example, if you were to begin explaining the rules of soccer to someone who had never seen a soccer game, the person would have a hard time understanding the rules. In this case, it would make sense to first show a video clip of a soccer game. Similarly, it would not be effective to describe the parts of a computer such as *disk drive* and *CPU* to someone who has never used a computer. It would be essential to have a computer in the classroom and point out each part as you describe it. When referring to a procedure or the characteristics of a piece of equipment or machinery, the learners must literally see what you mean.

Orderly in Space

Use this design for tasks that are visual in nature. For example, let's assume you are training employees to perform a quality inspection on shirts. You have brought ten shirts that did not pass a quality inspection to point out the flaws in each. To follow the orderly-in-space sequence, each shirt should be examined in the same order. If you begin by examining the collar, then the sleeves, then the front, and then the back of the first shirt, retain this pattern of observation for each shirt examined.

Avoid Vague Language

Be careful not to overuse terms that can be interpreted differently. Examples of vague language include the following:

fairly	might
mostly	perhaps
pretty much	possibly
somewhat	seems
sort of	frequently
a few	generally
a little	normally
a lot	often
some	probably
various	sometimes
may	usually

You cannot always avoid vague terms. To do so would distort the truth. However, try to be as clear as possible. If you know that a rule holds true 70 percent of the time, then state the 70 percent instead of saying that the rule applies most of the time.

❖ ❖ ❖

Applying the guidelines in this chapter will make your life as a trainer much easier. It can be exasperating when, after presenting what you thought was a thorough explanation of a topic, the learners' questions indicate that they are nowhere close to comprehension. Once you have identified the key points, you know what you need to emphasize, where you need examples, and where you need to incorporate a means for review. Developing a sequence will also be easier once the key points are actually written down. Key points can be emphasized in many ways. You can also add an element of interest to the training by using several ways to emphasize the key points.

PLANNING SHEET 5: MAKING EXPLANATIONS CLEAR

Key Points of the Lesson

_____

_____

_____

_____

_____

_____

_____

_____

_____

_____

Strategies for Emphasizing Key Points

_____

_____

_____

_____

_____

_____

_____

_____

_____

_____

_____

_____

Examples to Be Used

_____

_____

_____

_____

_____

_____

_____

_____

_____

_____

_____

Strategies for Periodic Review of Key Points

_____

_____

_____

_____

_____

_____

_____

_____

_____

_____

_____

_____

Organization/Sequence of Content

_____

_____

_____

_____

_____

_____

_____

_____

_____

_____

_____

_____

Vague Language to Avoid/Suggested Substitutes

_____

_____

_____

_____

_____

_____

_____

_____

_____

_____

_____

_____

CHAPTER SIX

ASKING AND ANSWERING QUESTIONS

The Astrologer

A long time ago, a man lived who gazed at the stars all night long. He believed that the stars revealed what the future would hold and he called himself an Astrologer.

One night, while he was out for a walk and gazing at the stars, he had a terrible premonition that the world would soon come to an end. Suddenly he realized he had just fallen into a hole full of mud and water. He frantically began to call for help. He was up to his ears in muddy water and the hole was so slippery that he slid back down each time he tried to climb out.

Finally a fellow villager came to his rescue. "My friend," said the villager, "what good is it to read the future in the stars if you cannot see what is at your feet?" Pay attention to what is right in front of you.

As trainers, it's tempting to predict what effect our instruction will have on the learners. It's easy to get so engrossed in presenting instruction that we lose sight of the reality of what's going on in the classroom. Probably everyone has had the experience of listening to a trainer drone on, totally oblivious to the class. These trainers rarely ask questions or allow others to ask them, but simply assume everything is fine. In reality, such people have no earthly idea whether or not the learners understand the points. Input from the learners actually makes a class more effective and more interesting.

Questions are powerful and essential teaching tools. You can use questions to stimulate discussion, check comprehension, learn about relevant experiences learners have had, and generate interest. Questions also help you keep on track and can be used to review or summarize key points. *How* you ask questions, ask for questions, and answer questions greatly affects the type and level of response you get.

Asking Questions

Several types of questions are available for your use as a trainer; a combination makes for a more interesting class. A definition of each basic type of question follows.

Developmental Questions

This type of question develops a point and is especially useful when your learners already have some knowledge about the subject. Developmental questions draw upon the background of your learners and allow them to learn from each others' experiences. For example, let's say you are teaching a course on stress management and have organized the topics to include the causes, symptoms, and ways to cope with stress. Rather than just telling your learners the points you want to make about each of those topics, it makes more sense to ask them about *their* experiences. Some sample developmental questions you might use are these: What situations do you find stressful? How can you tell when someone is stressed? What are some ways you deal with stress? The experiences they relate will develop at least some of the points you had intended to make, and the discussion will be more interesting to them because it reflects their own experiences.

Leading Questions

Leading questions are leading because they lead a learner to a reasonable answer. If you ask a question to someone who cannot answer it, follow up with a leading question instead of directing the original question to someone else. Leading questions can clarify the intent of your original question or give the learner a hint or clue to use. For instance, let's assume you ask a learner to name some situations that cause stress and the learner can't think of any. You might follow up with, "What times in your life did you feel extremely happy or extremely sad?" The learner could probably answer that. Leading questions cannot be planned in advance because they are constructed by taking into account the response of a specific learner.

Do not continue questioning a learner who is unable to answer a leading question. Leading questions are intended to build confidence; overused, they can make learners feel they've been put on the spot. If a learner cannot answer a leading question, ask the class in general or answer the question yourself.

Check Questions

Check questions test learner comprehension as you teach, ensuring that your learners stay with you. They are a means of reviewing key points and identifying learning difficulties. Ask check questions after you cover a critical or complex point. To be effective, a check question must be at the right level for your learners.

The learners should usually apply the information in some way and not simply recall information from memory. For example, if you have just explained how to compute employee pensions, effective check questions would require the learners to compute pension amounts for different situations. Solving a problem is a more effective check on learning than recalling the formula used to solve the problem. If some learners are unable to compute the pension correctly, spend more time explaining how to do it before moving on to another topic.

When teaching a hands-on task, a check question requires the learners to perform a portion of the task. This is especially important if the task requires several hours of practice before a learner will become proficient at it. Teaching someone how to drive is one example. Learners learning how to drive may at first practice just starting the car or just driving in reverse before they put it all together to drive any distance. Although driving is not a difficult task per se, it can be difficult from the perspective of someone learning it. At first it seems like there is a lot to remember. Frequent comprehension checks will prevent you from covering too much too fast. Even when the steps of a task are simple, the information is still new to the learners. At first, they will not remember everything they have been taught.

Effective check questions require some prior planning on your part. Ask yourself why you are asking a particular question. Reserve check questions for the more difficult or important aspects of your subject. Asking trivial questions is a waste of time and can be perceived as insulting by the learners. Have a clear purpose for each check question you use. For example, let's say that in your class on stress, you identified five major causes of stress. It would be of no value to ask "How many major causes of stress did we discuss today?" There is no way for the learners to use that information. It would make more sense to ask something like, "Give me some examples of the major causes of stress" and then ensure that learners indicate the cause of stress that the examples relate to.

Check questions can also build confidence in learners when they answer them correctly. They will gain a sense of satisfaction by answering a challenging but reasonable question. An effective question usually goes beyond asking learners to simply recall the information presented. When planning questions, design them to reflect realistic situations that require the learners to apply the information they are learning. An effective technique is to have learners come up with original applications of a concept you discussed. For example, in a class on dealing with irate customers, you might ask a learner to word the first sentence of a letter in response to a complaint. Other learners could then take turns adding additional sentences until the letter is complete.

Questions requiring sheer recall are of little value if the learners will have easy access to the information on the job. For instance, let's assume you are training learners how to compute employee benefits and they have a manual that contains the formulas used in these computations. A check question requiring a learner to state one of these formulas from memory would not serve any purpose.

Sometimes questions of recall are appropriate. They can be used to stress critical points, such as important safety precautions required when performing a task. If you choose to use a recall-type question, don't trivialize it with poor timing. If you state "always wear safety goggles when welding" and then immediately ask "what should you always wear while welding?" you have asked a simpleton question. It would be much more effective to wait until the end of the class and say you'd like to review the safety precautions. You could then ask learners to recall what they were.

Check questions help you teach at the right pace for your learners. This is especially important when you have material that snowballs—that is, the type of content where learners must use what they learned in one lesson in order to successfully complete the next lesson. If you wait too long before checking learner comprehension, you may find your learners have been lost from the start.

Rhetorical Questions

A rhetorical question is one that does not really require an answer. Rhetorical questions are used to underscore a point, such as "Who wants to live in poverty?" or to stimulate thought, for example, "What would you do if . . . ?" They can be effective ways to capture the learners' attention and are often used at the beginning of a class as an attention getter. Trainers also use rhetorical questions for transitions—moving from one point to the next—for example, "We've identified many causes of stress in our everyday life, but what can we do to cope?" When used as a transition, the rhetorical question will be answered—oftentimes by the trainer. The learners may also volunteer to comment. However, the question is asked in such a way that the learners realize the trainer doesn't expect an immediate response.

Poll Questions

A poll question asks for a show of hands regarding how many learners have either done something or are familiar with something. This type of question is used to learn about the background of the learners. It is also a way to personalize the instruction. For instance, in a class on XYZ computer spreadsheets, the trainer may ask, "How many of you have already used another type of computer spreadsheet?" or "How many of you are somewhat familiar with XYZ spreadsheets?" The trainer can follow up by asking learners with background in a particular area to share their experiences with the rest of the class. For example, "What kinds of things are you using it for at your company?" Poll questions are also good "energizers" and add interest to the class.

Questioning Techniques

Open-ended questions help get learners involved in a discussion. An open-ended question is one phrased so that it requires more than a one-word response. For example, instead of asking "Do you think that is a good idea?" you might ask "What do you think would happen if we did that?" Television talk show hosts are adept at the use of open-ended questions. If you listen to how they word their questions, you will notice they use phrases such as "How is it that . . . ?" "What are your views on . . . ?" "What is your reaction to . . . ?" "Tell me about your experience working with . . . " "What do you think would happen if we . . . ?" and so on.

Using Open-Ended Questions

You may first use a poll-type question (for example, "How many of you have experience with . . . ?" and then follow up with an open-ended question such as "What do you think of it?" When learners have relevant background experiences, several can respond to the same question. After one learner answers an open-ended question, be sure to see if anyone else has a comment to make. Remember to ask: "Are there any other thoughts on that?" or "Would anyone else like to comment?"

Keeping Questions Clear and Concise

You have probably seen instances in which learners were confused by trainer questions. Learners must understand what you're asking. Don't ask a question about material your learners haven't yet learned. (An exception to this is when you have some learners with expertise related to your subject.) Avoid technical terms or jargon that learners are not likely to know. Limit each question to one point. Multiple questions can be intimidating. Break down lengthy questions into more than one and let different learners answer.

Have a Reason for Asking Each Question. Questions should be used to develop key points, check comprehension, or stimulate discussion. Do not ask "simpleton" questions that insult the intelligence of your learners. Questions that can be answered yes or no often fall into the simpleton category, such as "Is it important to make a good first impression on a job interview?" Do not use questions to quiz learners on trivial points or on information that they can easily extract from their reference material. If you had given your learners a pamphlet listing the number of calories found in common foods, it would of be little value to ask "How many calories are in an apple?"

Use the Ask-Pause-Call-Evaluate Sequence. This means *ask* the question first, *pause* to allow learners time to think about it, *call* on a learner after the pause, and *evaluate* the response after the learner has given an answer:

Ask. As a general rule, address the question to the entire group. This way all of the learners will formulate an answer. You also avoid putting someone on the spot this way.

Pause. Some learners take longer than others to think about the questions you ask; others are ready to answer right away. Get in the habit of waiting about five seconds before you call on a learner to answer. Otherwise, those who take a little longer will not be able to volunteer.

Call. Select a learner to answer your question. If the question has more than one possible answer (for example, how can we cope with stress?), have more than one learner address the same question. Watch the nonverbal signals your learners send in response to a question. For example, a learner who immediately looks down after you ask a question most likely does not want to be called upon and you should respect that. If you see several confused looks, rephrase the question.

Do not call on learners in any set pattern, such as moving up and down rows. Remember, you want everyone to think about the questions you ask and to have ample time to formulate an answer. For the same reason, don't get into a routine of having the entire class answer your questions as a group.

Call on learners so that your questions are evenly distributed. Everyone should have the opportunity to participate. Sometimes you may have an overzealous learner who wants to answer most of the questions. When this happens, say, "Let's hear from someone we haven't heard from yet."

Evaluate. A learner should get immediate feedback after answering a question. If the question has a clearly defined right answer and the learner answers correctly, let the learner know the answer is correct.

I have seen trainers get the right answer from one learner and then immediately address the same question to another learner. That technique can imply that the first answer was incorrect. I have also seen trainers get the right answer from one learner and then immediately address a different question to another learner. The learner who answered first is left wondering why the trainer didn't comment.

Be sincere when giving positive feedback to a correct answer. Don't always use the same words. A trainer who always said "outstanding!" in response to a correct answer would soon be perceived as patronizing. There are many different ways you can let a learner know he or she is right.

Not all answers can be evaluated as being correct or incorrect. When you are asking a question of opinion or a question related to a learner's personal experience, you should acknowledge the response but not evaluate it. The point is not to let a learner's comment just drop as if it hadn't been made. Sometimes simply repeating an answer to this type of question is sufficient. For example, perhaps you asked "What are the characteristics of a good supervisor?" and a learner said "A good supervisor does not show favoritism." By repeating back "does not show favoritism" you have acknowledged the response. After acknowledging that response, you could then ask "What else?" If you were to ask this without first acknowledging the initial response, you would give the impression that the initial response had little merit.

One technique that is often used with broad discussion-type questions is to list the learners' ideas on newsprint or on a chalkboard. "What are the characteristics of a good supervisor?" is the sort of question that lends itself to this technique because there are many possible answers to it. When using this technique, be sure to write down *all* responses. Otherwise you will communicate that only the ideas you write down are important.

There will be times when you ask a question looking for a specific answer and get an answer that simply is wrong. Although you should not acknowledge an incorrect answer as correct, you need to be diplomatic when evaluating the learner's response. Your first course of action is to follow up an incorrect response with a leading question or hint that the learner can use to arrive at the right answer. For instance, let's assume you are teaching English grammar and ask the learner to name the indirect object in the sentence "The coach gave the team instructions." The learner answers "instructions." A possible leading question is "Who is the receiver of something in this sentence?" A similar approach is to give a hint: "'Instructions' is the *direct* object."

Another way to respond to an incorrect answer is to use the learner's response as an example of something related to what you're teaching. If you ask a learner to give an example of a simile and the learner says "The cat's eyes were jewels," you can say, "You have given an excellent example of a metaphor. A metaphor talks about one thing as if it were something else. Remember, a simile always uses the word 'like' or 'as' to indicate the likeness between two things." Responding in this way is much more effective than saying "No, that's not a simile." Do not flatly tell a learner that he or she is wrong. That only encourages defensive behavior and discourages further participation.

Try to find some merit in the response. If the learner is partially right, you can use phrases like "that's part of it," "you're on the right track," "you're close," or the like. Begin by saying what's right about the answer. If a teacher asks a learner, "What are the three primary colors?" and the learner answers "red, yellow and green," the teacher could say "Red and yellow are right." This is better than simply calling on another learner to answer the same question. The teacher might follow up with a hint, such as "Green is made up of yellow and one other primary color," which may lead the learner to correctly answer "blue."

When a learner is *completely* off track with an answer, it's important to find out the source of the confusion. It could be that your question was misinterpreted; perhaps it wasn't clear what you were really asking. If you believe this is the case, say "Let me rephrase that question" and ask it in a different way. On the other hand, if a learner gives a terrible answer to a clearly worded question, you must diplomatically let the learner know that the answer is incorrect. Do not be negative. Just the intonation in your voice can determine whether your response is positive or negative. Saying no with a pleasant intonation is much more effective than saying no with a note of impatience in your voice. You can also make an empathetic comment, such as "I know this can be confusing at first." If other learners are also unable to answer the question, then it's time to reteach the concept related to the question you asked.

If it appears that just one learner is lost, get with that learner on an individual basis to clear up the confusion.

Answering Questions

Part of teaching is asking the learners if they have questions they would like to ask of you. Some learners will not ask questions unless invited to do so.

How to Ask for Questions

It's not enough to periodically ask "Does everyone understand?" or "Are you with me?" because many learners will not want to admit they are not following the material. You will get a better response if you ask learners if they have any questions. Just how often you do this depends on how difficult your subject is to learn and how you have organized the material. Asking for questions about every fifteen to twenty minutes is a good rule of thumb. If you wait until the end of the class, it may be too late. Learners may have forgotten the questions they had earlier or may be confused beyond your ability to help them. I once observed a class in which the trainer did not ask for questions until the very end of the training. One learner commented that he had been totally lost.

An unanswered question can become a distraction in the mind of a learner. Learners can be so concerned with a question that they dwell on it and tune out the rest of the class. Get in the habit of noticing your learners' facial expressions. If you see puzzled looks or looks of obvious disagreement with a point, ask if there are any questions or comments at that point. If you notice one learner in particular, you can say, "You look like you might have a question."

How Not to Ask for Questions

Learners will not ask questions if you in any way communicate that you really don't want to be asked. The way you answer the first question asked of you will be carefully observed by the others. Here are some typical ways that trainers discourage questions:

- Making comments about a lot of material to be covered in a relatively short length of time.
- Asking for questions in a way that implies only idiots would have them: "I realize this is pretty self-explanatory material but are there any questions?" "The concepts we have covered are very simple but do you have any questions?"
- Asking for questions right before a scheduled break, lunch, or dismissal time for the day. Learners realize that asking at such times will annoy most other learners.
- Asking for questions and, seeing that there are none, saying "Good!"
- Prefacing an answer to a question with "As I stated earlier" or a similar phrase that implies the learner had not been paying attention.
- Looking at notes or materials instead of the learner who is asking the question.
- Interrupting a learner to answer the question before it has been fully stated. This often results in trainers addressing something other than what the learner had in mind.
- Brushing a learner off, such as by giving an abrupt answer rather than taking the time necessary to give a thorough answer.
- Frowning, looking at one's watch, or otherwise appearing impatient to get on with the rest of the class.
- Not pausing after asking for questions ("Any questions? Then let's move on to . . .")

Here are some techniques to encourage questions:

- Tell the learners from the start that you want them to ask questions. You can either tell them to ask at any time or tell them you have scheduled question-and-answer sessions throughout the training.
- Use statements such as "That's a good question." "I'm glad you asked that." "Your question brings up an important point." Be sincere. Don't use these when you get a truly off-the-wall question.

- Check to see if the answer you gave was helpful: "Does that answer your question?" "Does that help?" If the learner is still confused, make arrangements to get with him or her individually.
- If you get a question about material you plan to cover later, give a brief answer anyway. Then state that this will be explained in more detail later. Don't just say "You're getting ahead" or "We'll talk about that later."
- Look directly at the learner who is asking the question.
- Be patient. Respond positively to questions.
- If you don't know the answer to a question, say so! Then tell the learner you will research it. Remember to follow through on your commitment and inform the class of what you find out.
- Make sure you understand what the learner is asking. If you're not sure, paraphrase the question and ask if you understood it correctly.
- Be sure everyone heard the question. Oftentimes learners sitting toward the front of the class will not project their voices so that everyone can hear. Ask if everyone heard the question. If not, state it again before answering.
- Listen carefully to the kinds of questions you get. If questions from more than one learner indicate a total lack of understanding of something, it is probably a sign that you need to reteach that point before going on to the next.
- After you answer one learner's question, ask if anyone else has a question. Sometimes trainers ask for questions, answer one, and then immediately resume lecturing. There's a good chance that if one learner has a question so do others.

◆ ◆ ◆

The questions you ask are valuable tools to you as a trainer. Developmental questions generate learner involvement and allow you to draw upon the experiences learners have had relevant to the training. Check questions let you know how well the learners are comprehending the material. Leading questions can build learners' confidence by allowing them to answer a question they originally thought they couldn't answer. Rhetorical and poll questions are a means of adding variety and interest. To be effective, questions must be worded clearly and in a way that encourages learners to share their thoughts

The questions learners ask of you are equally valuable. The fact that they are asking tells you they are interested. The type of questions they ask can provide you cues regarding what content needs to be reviewed and what is important to them. Always respond to learners' questions in a way that will encourage other learners to ask questions as well.

PLANNING SHEET 6: QUESTIONS

Developmental Questions to Use

_____

_____

_____

_____

_____

_____

_____

_____

_____

_____

Check Questions to Use

_____

_____

_____

_____

_____

_____

_____

_____

_____

_____

Rhetorical Questions to Use

_____

_____

_____

_____

_____

_____

_____

_____

_____

_____

_____

_____

Poll Questions to Use

_____

_____

_____

_____

_____

_____

_____

_____

_____

_____

_____

_____

_____

Points to Stop and Ask for Questions

_____

_____

_____

_____

_____

_____

_____

_____

_____

_____

Techniques to Encourage Responses

_____

_____

_____

_____

_____

_____

_____

_____

_____

_____

CHAPTER SEVEN

POLISHING COMMUNICATIONS SKILLS

The Musician

A music student delighted in playing the harp. He had never heard anyone else play the harp yet he believed that no music could be more beautiful than when he played. He was so convinced of this that he arranged to give a concert in a large theater. But the audience at his concert was accustomed to hearing accomplished harp players. When the musician began to play, the audience chased him off the stage and banned him from ever coming back again. Listen through ears other than your own.

Although instructors are not performers, they still need effective personal presentation skills to gain and maintain the interest of the learners. These are the same skills taught in public speaking classes. Like a speech, a training session requires an effective introduction and an effective conclusion. The old rule "Know what you are going to say first and know what you are going to say last" applies to training sessions as well as speeches.

The Introduction

The first five minutes of a class are critical because that's when the learners decide whether or not they are going to invest their attention in the training. (An introduction is different from an icebreaker; the latter is a preclass activity used to establish a positive and comfortable learning atmosphere, the former is the beginning of the lesson.) A sample introduction appears on page 134. The entire introduction should take about five minutes and contain the following items.

The Attention Getter

The purpose of an attention getter is to focus the learner's attention on the topic of the lesson. To teach anyone anything, you must first have that person's attention! Here are some techniques you can use to gain attention.

- Share a personal experience or ask learners to relate an experience.
- Ask a rhetorical question, such as "What would you do if . . . ?" or "How many times has this happened to you . . . ?"
- Tell an (inoffensive!) joke or show a transparency of a humorous cartoon related to the topic.
- Ask a poll-type question—a show of hands by all who have experienced or witnessed the discussion subject.
- Relate an interesting statistic or fact.
- Show a brief clip of a videotape.
- Conduct a short role play.

The technique you choose should depend on the topic and the learners' background. If your lesson is on a serious or emotional topic such as child abuse, you certainly would not use humor in the attention getter. Stating statistics related to the topic would be appropriate in such a case. Likewise, if you're teaching the XYZ computer program to novices, it may or may not work to ask, "How does your department plan to use the XYZ computer program?" Whatever technique you use, remember that the attention getter must relate to the subject to be effective.

Motivation Statement

The learners want to know how this lesson will be useful to them. Why is it important? How is it relevant? How and when will they use the information? The answers to these questions aren't always obvious. When I taught an instructor-training course, many learners initially did not see the relationship of being able to write learning objectives to being able to teach a class. They came eager to begin presenting practice classes and hadn't given much thought to learning how to carefully plan the classes. If I hadn't first explained why they needed to learn how to write learning objectives, they probably would have thought they'd come to the wrong course.

Effective motivation statements tell the learners *specifically* how they will benefit from the training. Perhaps their work will be easier or they will save time by learning more efficient procedures. Perhaps learning a new skill will make them more competitive when they are being considered for a promotion. Perhaps the skill they are learning has applications in their personal lives as well as on the job—required CPR training, for example ("Imagine if one of your family members suddenly started choking. There's no describing the difference between immediately knowing what to do and the panic of hoping help arrives in time"). If there's more than one benefit, state them all.

If possible, stress the positive benefits from applying the learning as opposed to the negative consequences of not applying the learning. For example, it would be better to state how learning a new skill will make the learners' work easier instead of saying that the learners will no longer be competitive workers if they don't learn this skill. There will be times when stating the negative consequences of not being able to apply the learning will be unavoidable; when teaching CPR, for example, one would have to state how the patient could be adversely affected if the techniques were not properly applied.

During the first few minutes of a training session, the learners are going to decide how much attention they are going to invest. An effective motivation statement will generate learner interest and active participation.

Learning Objectives

Learning objectives (as discussed in Chapter Two) are the cornerstone of the training. They form the basis for everything that follows: the content, methods, media, and evaluation of the overall effectiveness of the training. As learning objectives indicate the intent of the training, they must be discussed with the learners. If you are using a traditional learning objective with the three parts of action, condition, and standard, you must clearly present all three. For example:

You will perform CPR (action) on a training mannequin (condition). To be certified in this task, you must be able to get the indicator light on the mannequin to come on within five minutes of beginning the CPR (standard).

If you are not teaching the type of task that requires a formal evaluation, you can modify the learning objective. However, it still needs to be stated in specific terms. For example, "today you will practice writing performance evaluations that stress employee accomplishments. You will be working on case studies in small groups. Each group will write a performance evaluation on the employee described in its case study. We will review each case study and you can share your ideas with each other" is preferable to "today we are going to discuss performance appraisals." Learning objectives are stated so that learners know exactly what to expect from the onset of the training.

Overview of the Lesson

This is a preview of what is to come. It is a brief summary of how the time will be spent. Mention about how much time will be spent on major topics and any special activities, such as viewing a videotape, going to a computer lab, or the like. Overviews are especially important when the context of the training is going to change. For example, learners in a first aid course can plan what days they definitely need to wear casual clothes because of the specific tasks they will be practicing. A learner attending a course that will feature a guest speaker may wish to bring a tape recorder on that day. If the training requires any assignments of the learners, an overview can help them plan their time.

Learners are always curious about what the training is going to be like. An overview satisfies that curiosity so that they can focus on the training instead of wondering what is coming up next.

Relationship of Lesson to Past and Future Training

If the lesson is part of a course, it is helpful to show how one lesson relates to or builds upon another. For example, in a training session on conducting a job search you might say, "Today you will learn how to write a resume. Tomorrow you will learn how to identify the questions an employer is likely to ask you based upon your resume. You will also learn the most common questions that employers ask and how to respond to them. Then on Friday, we will conduct mock interviews to give you practice explaining your qualifications and answering possible employer questions."

The Conclusion

The conclusion contains the following items.

Final Questions

Although you will be asking for questions throughout the lesson, it's important to see if there are any final questions before you close. Be sure that you ask for them in a way that projects that you are genuinely interested in answering any questions the learners may have. Also, if a learner does have a question at this time, be sure to ask if anyone else has further questions before beginning your summary.

Summary

Provide a brief review of what the lesson contained. Do not simply name the topics covered, such as: "We discussed chronological and functional résumés." Restate between four and six key ideas. If confusion surfaced earlier about a certain concept, be sure to recap that particular concept as part of the summary. Another technique is to ask a check question geared toward key points contained in the lesson. Remember that check questions should require the learners to apply the information they have learned and not simply parrot a point you stated earlier.

Closing Statement

A closing statement ties a ribbon around the package. It cues the learners that the instruction is over and prevents an ending that simply fizzles out. An effective closing statement is positive and directly relates to the motivation statement. For example, if the lesson had been on CPR, the motivation statement may have been: "You never know when a friend or family member could begin choking on a piece of food. If this happened and you were the only person around, would you be able to save a life?" The closing statement would then be something like: "Now, if you find yourself in an emergency situation where someone needs CPR, you will not stand by with a desperate feeling of helplessness. You know how to administer CPR and you are able to save a life."

A Note on Planning the Introduction and Conclusion

Planning means knowing ahead of time the points you are going to make. *It does not mean writing a script and memorizing it.* You must be natural to be effective. Never attempt to memorize word-for-word what you plan to say—this results in a mechanical, "canned" style.

Effective verbal and nonverbal communications skills are essential to the teaching-learning process. The best way to improve your skills is to watch yourself conducting a class on videotape. You will learn things about yourself that you otherwise would never have known.

The Monkey and the Camel

All the animals of the Kingdom were gathered for a grand party. The Monkey was chosen to perform an exquisite dance. The Monkey danced with such agility and grace that everyone applauded wildly. The Camel became very envious of the Monkey and yearned for the same recognition. So he decided that he too would dance. However, he did not have the Monkey's talent and he groped about looking both ridiculous and grotesque. The animals were so insulted by his performance that they told him he would never again be invited to one of their parties. It is absurd to ape our betters.

Verbal Skills

The most important rule of effective communication is: Be yourself! Converse with the learners; don't talk at them. You are not on the stage. Beyond that, use the following checklist to enhance your verbal skills.

Articulation

Articulate. Simply put, this means be clear and distinct. Don't mumble, slur words, or run them together. Say the entire word; don't drop off endings—for example, "goin' " instead of "going." Avoid chopping up your speech. Speak in complete sentences. Finish one thought before going on to the next.

Conversational Tone

Learning involves dialogue. When you converse with friends or family, you certainly don't speak in a monotone. The inflection of your voice is varied. These changes in pitch or tone help punctuate speech, placing question marks and exclamation points where they belong. There is *energy* in your voice. Why should you speak any differently as a trainer? Voice variety is a major factor in maintaining interest and attention. No one wants to listen to dull, monotone speech.

Reading Aloud

Don't read or have learners take turns reading portions of text aloud to the class. We put our children to sleep by reading to them and reading aloud to learners tends to have the same effect! Having the learners read aloud is often associated with grade school classrooms and may insult people in addition to boring them.

Grammar

Watch your grammar. Unfortunately, you can lose credibility quickly by making grammatical errors. Along the same lines, don't overuse slang expressions. The use of incorrect grammar and slang can convey that you are less knowledgeable than you really are. In my experience, people who make grammatical errors typically make the same type of error repeatedly, such as confusing the use of don't and doesn't. It's not that they need to relearn *all* of the rules. Brushing up on a few grammar rules is well worth the effort.

Vocabulary

Use vocabulary appropriate to the learners' background. Explain any technical terms they have not yet encountered. Avoid pompous language, such as "the importance of which cannot be exaggerated." Again, be yourself and use the same level of vocabulary with the learners that you use with your friends.

Fillers

Don't overuse fillers. Fillers are words and phrases used to fill or pad speech. We use them as we pause trying to think of what to say next. Sometimes we use them as an indication that we are going on to a new thought. Common fillers are "okay," "ah," "um," "you know," "you see," "actually," "anyhow," "basically," "and so forth," and "like." Overusing fillers distracts listeners. They wait for the next filler to come. I've seen learners actually make tally marks of the number of "okays" a trainer used.

Volume

Adjust your volume to the size of the group. Be sure you are easily heard, but don't shout at the group. A loud voice is a monotone voice because there's no room for ups and downs. Get a microphone if you're addressing a large group. If you're not sure if your volume is comfortable to others, ask them!

Pace

Keep a pace that's fast enough to be interesting but slow enough to allow for note-taking. An effective pace comes with practice. Most people speak at the rate of 120 to 150 words per minute, but there is no standard acceptable rate. Slow, drawn-out speech is monotonous and boring, however, and machine-gun delivery is frustrating to learners being exposed to an idea for the first time. The pace should be varied just like the tone of voice. Slow down for complex and crucial ideas. Look at the group—if you see several people frantically writing, pause a few seconds before going on. Pauses are also a way to give emphasis to an idea. An intentional pause following a critical idea is a cue for learners to reflect upon that idea.

Pronunciation

Use correct pronunciation. When in doubt, consult the dictionary. Pronouncing words incorrectly can erode your credibility much the same as using incorrect grammar. Don't worry about having a regional accent. That's part of being yourself. It can even be an advantage. Others may find it interesting since it's different from what they're used to hearing. You most likely can't change it anyway and you'd sound artificial if you tried.

Nonverbal Skills

Use the following checklist to improve your nonverbal skills.

Eye Contact

Make direct eye contact with the people in the group. Sometimes nervous trainers avoid eye contact with individuals. They look at the wall, the floor, their notes—anything but other people! They not only miss the nonverbal feedback the learners provide, they also communicate that they are not interested in dialogue. The learners may as well be listening to tape.

Always look at someone who is speaking to you. When a learner is asking a question or making a comment and the trainer is looking down at notes instead of at that person, what does that communicate?

When you are speaking, make direct eye contact with everyone at some point. Your eye contact should be evenly distributed and natural. "Eye dart," or looking like a nervous rabbit rapidly glancing from one person to the next, is unnatural. So is looking at the same person for more than a few seconds unless you are responding to his or her question or comment. Everyone should feel included when you speak. Don't only look at selected people. Note: seating arrangement can affect eye contact. Avoid situations where the majority of the group is seated on one side of the room. It's easy to focus eye contact on the side where the majority of people are seated and forget about the others.

Movement

Imagine watching a television talk show where the camera angle never changes. The show wouldn't seem nearly as interesting. The same principle applies to a training session. If you stand during the training session, don't let your feet grow roots! Move around. Physical distance can be associated with psychological distance. Always staying at the front of the room builds a psychological barrier between you and the learners. You will be perceived as more open and approachable if you move near the learners.

Your range of movement is determined by the classroom setup. If you are addressing a large group in a traditional classroom setup, you can move from one side of the room to the other more easily than you can move down into the group. If you move down into the group you have your back to those seated in front, and you don't want to be speaking with your back to anyone. Movement must have purpose. It makes sense to move to the side of the room where a person who just asked a question is seated. It makes sense to move to a chalkboard to use it. It does not make sense to pace back and forth just to be moving. If you move from one side of the room to the other, stay there a few minutes before moving back. Constant motion projects that you are nervous. Effective movement is automatic and natural.

Gestures

Keep your gestures natural. Gestures are the movement of arms and hands to punctuate speech; we all use them in everyday conversation without thinking about them. They blend naturally with our unique styles of speaking. Do not try to plan your gestures. Rehearsed gestures communicate a lack of sincerity. Gestures are spontaneous and take care of themselves. When using a pointer at a screen, remember to set it down once you have finished using it; otherwise you'll look like you're conducting a band. Never use a pointer to recognize a learner with a raised hand.

Facial Expressions

Be aware of your facial expressions. The face and the eyes are the focus of human communication. The expression on your face will be noticed by the learners. Just as a monotone voice is dull and uninteresting, so is a stone-faced demeanor. Again, the rule "be yourself" cannot be overemphasized. If you like people and like the subject for the training, this should automatically show on your face! I have encountered people who believed that if they smiled or in any way looked pleasant, the learners wouldn't take them seriously. This idea didn't take them very far as trainers.

Habits or Mannerisms

Avoid annoying habits or mannerisms. Often an outlet for nervousness, they can really detract from a trainer's effectiveness. People who observe themselves on videotape often are amazed, never before realizing that they had particular mannerisms. Constantly jingling keys or change in one's pocket, holding a pen and clicking it throughout the entire class, cracking gum, constantly toying with one's hair or pushing it off of one's face are just a few examples of ways to drive learners crazy. If you are new to speaking in front of a group, videotape yourself giving a presentation. There is absolutely no substitute for watching yourself on videotape as a means to improve your presentation skills. Nothing else comes close to enabling you to see yourself as others see you.

Many of the poor communications skills just mentioned are actually attempts to cope with nervousness. Avoiding eye contact, a monotone voice, and constant mannerisms are typical of nervous trainers. Everyone experiences some degree of nervousness before teaching a class. Actually, this is good—you feel some anxiety because you *care* about doing a good job.

The Fox and the Lion

A Fox, upon seeing a Lion for the very first time, trembled with fear. Never before had he experienced such fright. A few days later, he encountered the Lion again. Although he was still frightened, he didn't feel as terrified as he did the first time he had seen the Lion. The following day, he saw the Lion again. This time he said, "Hello, my friend! It's good to see you! Will you join me for lunch?" Acquaintance softens prejudices.

Nervousness

Like anything else, conducting training gets easier with practice. The more classes you teach, the more confident you will become. Beginning with an icebreaker has an added benefit of helping you to feel more comfortable as well as setting the tone for a positive learning environment.

A very common experience is for the trainer to begin the class feeling extremely nervous but to calm down considerably after the first five or ten minutes. Eliciting learner participation early on is another way to break the ice. Ask for opinions or relevant experiences from the learners as part of your introduction to the material. One reason you feel nervous is because you don't know how the learners are reacting. Once you get feedback, it's easier to relax. When you spot learners who give you positive nonverbal feedback, such as smiling at you or nodding heads in agreement with what you're saying, look at those people for reassurance for the first few minutes. Do this only for a few minutes as a technique to help you relax; at some point you must distribute your eye contact to everyone.

The best prescription for nervousness is preparation. Learners respect trainers who are obviously prepared. Checking out the room and equipment ahead of time, reviewing any handouts, slides, or transparencies for accuracy, and making sure you have all of the materials and supplies you need will prevent many potential problems. A critical part of preparation is to develop a lesson plan. It can serve as your security blanket because it indicates exactly what you are going to do in a step-by-step fashion. Should you have a temporary memory lapse, you can glance at your lesson plan and recapture your thought. Chapter Nine shows you how to develop a lesson plan.

PLANNING SHEET 7

The Introduction:

ATTENTION GETTER

_____

_____

_____

_____

_____

MOTIVATION STATEMENT

_____

_____

_____

_____

_____

_____

LEARNING OBJECTIVES

_____

_____

_____

_____

_____

_____

_____

LESSON OVERVIEW

_____

_____

_____

_____

_____

RELATIONSHIP OF LESSON TO PAST/FUTURE TRAINING

_____

_____

_____

_____

_____

The Conclusion:

FINAL QUESTIONS

_____

_____

SUMMARY

_____

_____

_____

_____

_____

_____

CLOSING STATEMENT

_____

_____

_____

_____

_____

VERBAL SKILLS I MAY NEED TO IMPROVE

_____

_____

_____

_____

_____

NONVERBAL SKILLS I MAY NEED TO IMPROVE

_____

_____

_____

_____

_____

WAYS TO FIGHT NERVOUSNESS

_____

_____

_____

_____

CHAPTER EIGHT

ENHANCING INTERPERSONAL SKILLS

The Fox and the Stork

A Fox prepared a savory pot of soup and was about to sit down to dinner when his neighbor, a Stork, came by for a visit. The Fox, not really wanting to share his dinner, pretended to be hospitable by pouring some soup in a large flat dish and offering it to the Stork. He knew very well that the Stork, with her long bill, would not be able to partake.

The Fox ate bowl after bowl while the poor Stork was unable to get a single drop. When the Fox had finally finished eating, the Stork said, "Do come to my house for dinner tomorrow. I'm preparing stew, which I know is your favorite dish."

When the Fox went to have dinner with the Stork the next day, she served the stew in a pitcher with a long and narrow neck. Now it was the Fox's turn to try in vain to get a single morsel while the Stork ate enough for both of them. Treat others as you wish to be treated.

It has been my general experience that learners respond to trainers according to the way they perceive they are being treated. If they perceive the trainer as being personable, they will respond in a personable way. If they perceive negative qualities in the trainer, they are likely to become either apathetic or hostile. Realize this: everything you do will be echoed back to you in one way or another. You will get back what you give.

Effective teachers and trainers relate well to learners. If I were asked to list the three most important traits related to trainer excellence, good interpersonal skills would be one of them (the other two would be the ability to clearly explain the subject and the ability to maintain learner interest and attention). What exactly are interpersonal skills?

Interpersonal refers to relationships with people. Traits that foster relating well to people include friendliness, warmth, approachability, enthusiasm, a sense of humor, and patience. Traits that do *not* foster relating well to people include arrogance, inflexibility, insensitivity, sarcasm, one-upmanship, and a need to be in charge.

Interpersonal skills affect how well learners meet the training objectives. For example, learners are unlikely to ask questions of a trainer who they have seen brush off someone else's question. In this case they will leave the training with unanswered questions. Training that involves introducing a major change in the workplace can actually generate resistance to the change if the trainer has poor interpersonal skills. Imagine a domineering trainer explaining how the company's new total quality management system will incorporate everyone's input!

Unfortunately, people with poor interpersonal skills do not always realize how they are perceived by others. How many arrogant people do you know who would describe themselves as arrogant? It's tough to precisely describe how to acquire good interpersonal skills. Listed below are basic guidelines for trainers, which should at least provide a good start.

Be Yourself

When I was teaching a trainer training course, I was amazed at the number of people who felt they had to assume a different personality when they taught a class. Perhaps they were imitating the style of a former trainer they had known. There is no universal teacher's personality! You will only project that you are insincere if you try to become someone else when you teach. Even if you found the style of a former trainer to be highly effective, remember you are not that person.

Use Names

Call people by their names. Provide everyone with a five-by-seven index card and have them fold the cards in half horizontally. Give them thick felt-tip markers to use to print their names on the cards. Have them stand up the folded cards like a tent so you will be able to see the names.

Watch Nonverbals

Respond to the nonverbal communication of learners. Facial expressions, eye contact, nodding or shaking one's head, yawning, leaning forward, fidgeting, gathering up one's books to leave, crossing one's arms are all examples of nonverbal communication.   What are the learners telling you by their nonverbal communication? You will often be able to sense that someone is confused or disagrees with something you said simply by that person's facial expression. If you notice such a look, respond to it: "John, you look like you have a question," or "Mary, I get the feeling you don't go along with that." A common problem I have seen is trainers who are completely oblivious when a class is nonverbally *screaming* for a break. Get in the habit of looking at people as well as listening to them. Otherwise, you will miss out on an important part of the communication process.

The Man and the Lion

A Man and a Lion were traveling together on a trip. They began to discuss the traits of strength and courage. They each believed these traits to be of the utmost importance. Their discussion became heated when each claimed to be superior to the other in strength and courage. They continued to argue about who was superior until they came upon a statue of a Man strangling a Lion. "There's proof that men are stronger than lions!" said the Man with great conviction. "That's only your opinion," said the Lion. "If Lions could make statues, I assure

you that you would see the Man underneath!" There are two sides to every question.

Make Time for Questions

The perspective and perception of the learners can be surprising to you but nonetheless must be respected. It's surprising to me when trainers seem irritated when learners ask them questions or (oh horrors) disagree with them. Comments such as "Yes, as I said before . . . " or "I don't know how to make it any simpler" do not encourage a positive learning environment. Neither does looking at your watch when being asked a question, interrupting a learner who is asking a question, or giving an abrupt answer. If just one learner appears totally confused, offer to get with that person individually after class or on break.

Give No Offense

Avoid offensive language and jokes. If you're not sure whether a specific word or joke is offensive, don't use it! Even otherwise astute politicians have gotten themselves into trouble in this area. A subject that tends to evoke strong emotions in people or that is controversial in nature—politics, religion, and feminism, to name a few—should not be used as the subject of a joke. Never preface a joke with something like "If no one here is sensitive about (whatever topic), I have a joke for you." Just because a person doesn't speak up at that point does not mean the joke won't be perceived as offensive.

Be Gender Neutral

Use gender-neutral language. Don't make it sound as if only one gender exists. When using examples of people, include both males and females. Also, don't make statements that imply a person in a given occupation must be of one gender (such as "nurses are courageous women" or "the young men who compose today's Army"). Never assume that only one gender is knowledgeable about a particular topic. Call on people equally, regardless of the topic under discussion.

The North Wind and the Sun

The North Wind and the Sun were arguing over who was the stronger. They decided to settle their dispute by seeing who could be the first to get a traveler to shed his cloak. The North Wind tried first. With all the gust he could muster, he blew down so furiously upon the man that the man swirled around like a leaf spinning through the air. But all the while the man held onto his cloak all the tighter.

Next it was the Sun's turn. He cast some gentle rays at the man, causing him to feel just the slightest bit too warm. The man soon unfastened his cloak. Then the Sun gradually increased his rays, causing the man to hang the cloak loosely across his shoulders. The Sun continued to gradually increase the warmth until the man, with a great sigh of relief, threw his cloak off and contin-ued his journey in comfort. Persuasion is better than force.

Use Gentle Persuasion

Never argue with a learner. Doing so is a guaranteed no-win situation. Even if you prove yourself 100 percent correct you lose. The learner will lose face and will likely feel hostile toward you. Others may em-pathize with the one who challenged you and feel hostile as well.

Let's assume a learner says that an idea you suggested will never work. Instead of arguing, say something like "My experience has been . . . " There can be no argument about your personal experience. Also, try to find some merit in the learner's argument, perhaps saying some-thing like, "I agree that there can be exceptions to this, for example in the case of . . . " Another phrase that sometimes diffuses a potential ar-gument is, "I understand that's your opinion." Again, there's nothing to argue. If someone persistently challenges you, tell the person that you'll discuss it individually with him or her.

Respect the Learners

Establish an atmosphere of mutual respect. Confucius once said, "The process of teaching and learning stimulate each other. Teaching is half of learning." Recognize the value of the experience the learners bring with them. You can learn from them as much as they can learn from you. Your role as a trainer is one of service. Keep in mind that you are dealing with adults. Allow them input into the course. Let them make some decisions. Do as much as you can to ensure that the training is use-ful to them.

Use Diplomacy

Be diplomatic when reacting to behaviors you find irritating. You may encounter people who tend to create problems for the class—for example, the person who wants to dominate a conversation to the point that others give up trying to contribute. Another example is the person who keeps getting the group off track by bringing up irrelevant topics. Although this is frustrating for you, it's important to deal with these people diplomatically. Comments like "We still haven't heard from a lot of people" or "What other opinions do we have?" are certainly preferable to "Would you mind giving someone else a chance to speak?"

People who engage in these irritating behaviors are usually not intentionally being disruptive. They are often unaware of how their behavior is perceived by the group. However, if you do not respond in some way they are likely to continue. Your tone of voice and demeanor make all the difference in how effectively you respond to their behaviors. Sometimes it is necessary to interrupt the person who has gone off on a tangent: "Excuse me for interrupting, Jane, but I think we're really getting off track here. We still haven't finished discussing . . . "

If you should encounter a person you find to be extremely disruptive and the person doesn't respond to your comments in class, meet with this person privately. Tell the person specifically what your concern is and how you perceive it to be affecting you and the class. For example: "John, I've noticed in class that you're usually the first person to get the solution to the practice problems. Most of the others seem to need more time. I want everyone to work through each problem. I'm going to ask you not to volunteer your answer as soon as you get it so that I can make sure everyone works through each problem."

Be Professional

Professional trainers are well prepared to conduct the training and arrive on time. They ensure all materials are in good order—that is, legible and with no typographical errors. They avoid making derogatory comments about others and keep confidential information confidential. Most important, their actions reflect their genuine concern that the learners' needs be met. They don't disappear when learners are working on small-group activities. They are willing to stay after the session has officially ended and answer questions on an individual basis if necessary.

Keep a Sense of Humor

You don't have to be a comedian to have a sense of humor. Be able to laugh at yourself if the occasion presents itself. I once had a class that, knowing I often was unaware of the time, would change the classroom clock to make the class period a few minutes shorter. This went on for several periods before I caught on! I had to laugh. I've encountered learners who would say or do things that were absolutely silly. A few moments of silliness can be welcome at times.

Be Accessible

Talk with learners before and after class. Being present at these times communicates that you are approachable and do not view training as merely a job that can only occur when you are on the clock. Even if you just talk about the weather you are establishing rapport, and the learners are more likely to participate in class if they feel comfortable with you.

PLANNING SHEET 8: INTERPERSONAL SKILLS

Ideas for creating a positive learning environment

_____

_____

_____

_____

Habits to avoid

_____

_____

_____

Ways to personalize the session:

3x5 cards for name tents

_____

_____

Time to meet individually with learners

_____

_____

Other

_____

_____

_____

_____

CHAPTER NINE

DEVELOPING A LESSON PLAN

The Flute-Playing Wolf

A young Goat was out with his herd on a warm spring day. He closed his eyes while sunning himself and soon fell asleep. When he awoke, he saw a ferocious Wolf looking down at him and licking his lips. "Oh, please," the Goat cried, "before you eat me let me have one last wish." "And what might that be?" asked the Wolf. "Play your flute for me that I might dance," said the Goat.

The Wolf, who very much enjoyed playing the flute, decided to grant this request. As he played his flute, the Goat danced with great glee. This encouraged the Wolf to play louder and louder. A nearby pack of dogs, hearing the music, ran over to see who was playing the flute so loudly. When they saw the Wolf, they chased him away and the young Goat's life was spared.

"This is my own fault," said the Wolf. "I was playing the flute when I should have been hunting." Don't be distracted from what you set out to do.

Lesson plans keep you from being distracted. They keep training focused. A lesson plan is a document that includes all the essential information you need to conduct the training. This is where everything you have planned to do is put together in an organized fashion. (Refer to Planning Sheets 1–8 when developing your lesson plan.) Lesson plans are especially helpful to have on hand if someone else must conduct the training at the last minute in the event you become ill or have an emergency. Also, you will find them helpful if you only teach a specific class occasionally. Even though you know the subject well, having a lesson plan ensures that you don't leave out important information and that you present the material in a logical sequence for new learners.

When you are teaching, your attention is split in dozens of directions. In addition to the content of the instruction, you use various types of training aids, ask and answer questions, give directions for exercises or tests, try to remember to distribute your eye contact evenly among the learners, watch the learners' nonverbal communication, move around the classroom, and much more. Until you get comfortable with a lesson, it is very easy to lose track of where you are or to forget to do something, such as distributing one of the handouts. By periodically glancing down at your lesson plan, you can keep yourself organized and on track.

As always, consider the context of the training. Highly structured lesson plans are applicable to skill training where the trainer is clearly the subject matter expert and the learners have little or no background. If the trainer is assuming a nondirective role, the lesson plan should be modified accordingly. In this case not all elements may be applicable and the lesson plan could be loosely structured, perhaps consisting of general guidelines and suggestions for the trainer.

Although there is no set format for a lesson plan, most of them should include the types of information listed in the following two outlines. The annexes after that indicate what they should contain once developed. An abbreviated sample lesson plan follows the annexes; note that it provides an example of only one approach.

Administrative Information

1. Course title
2. Lesson title
3. Learning objective(s)
4. Personnel to be trained
5. Prerequisites (essential previous training)
6. Training aids, equipment and supplies
7. Method(s) of instruction
8. Examination information (directions to administer and score)
9. References
10. Special requirements

Lesson Plan Body

1. Introduction
   A. Focus attention on topic
   B. Motivation
   C. Learning objective(s)
   D. Overview of lesson
   E. Relationship of lesson to past and future training
2. Lesson content
   A. Detailed outline of topics
   B. Estimated time for each topic
   C. Instructions indicating when to use training aids
   D. Instructions indicating the type of method to use with each topic
   E. Notes to trainer
      (1) To remind yourself to ask learners if they have questions
      (2) To ask specific check questions at given points throughout the lesson
      (3) To summarize at given points throughout the lesson
      (4) To illustrate a concept on the chalkboard
      (5) To jot down learner ideas on the easel board

(6) To pass out a handout

(7) To conduct an in-class exercise at a given point

(8) To mention a safety precaution at a given point

(9) To give a break at a given point

3. Conclusion

   A. Final questions

   B. Summary

   C. Closure

Annexes

1. Instructions for preclass activities, such as icebreaker, polling of learner expectations, room arrangement

2. Photocopies of overhead transparencies

3. Copies of handouts provided to learners in sequential order

4. Other training aids

   A. List of 35mm slides

   B. Descriptions of easel charts to be prepared ahead of class

   C. Descriptions of video or audio tapes used

   D. Descriptions of computer screens to be projected during a slide show

5. Practice exercises

6. Tests

Sample Lesson Plan Format

1. Course title: Personal Management Skills
2. Lesson title: Stress Management
3. Learning objectives:
   A. State major causes of stress
   B. Identify effects of unchecked stress
   C. Describe techniques to manage stress
4. Personnel to be trained: Company XYZ customer service representatives
5. Prerequisites: none
6. Training aids, equipment and supplies
   A. Easel board and markers
   B. Videotape player, twenty-seven-inch monitor
   C. Three-by-five-inch index cards
7. Methods of instruction
   A. Conference
   B. Case study exercise
8. Examination information: not applicable
9. Learner materials: *Coping with Stress* manual developed by Company XYZ Training Department
10. Special requirements
    A. Limit class size to twenty
    B. Learners will be divided into four small groups during an exercise; ensure classroom allows for this

Lesson Content

Note: introduce self and conduct icebreaker and learner expectations exercises at Annex A.

Note: review the following administrative information:

Location of restrooms

Location of telephones

Availability of coffee and refreshments

Scheduled time for lunch break

Planned breaks; encourage learners to indicate if they need more often or sooner

Introduction

I. Focus learner attention on topic

Ask for examples of stressful situations learners have recently experienced. Obtain several different examples.

II. Motivation

Ask several learners to describe how stress affects them. *Note:* record responses on easel board.

Explain that although stress cannot be eliminated from our lives, it can be managed. Emphasize the benefits of managing stress.

III. Objectives

Note: write on easel board.

The objectives of this class are for you to learn (1) what causes stress, (2) how to identify symptoms of stress, (3) the effects of unmanaged stress, and (4) techniques you can use to relieve stress.

IV. Overview of lesson

This morning we will discuss the causes, symptoms, and effects of stress. Because people experience stress in different ways, I'd like to show you a twenty-minute videotape that shows a number of very different but typical symptoms of stress. We will finish the morning with a discussion of the many different causes of stress. I have brought with me a few case histories that I think you will find interesting. After lunch, we will focus on ways to manage stress. This will include practicing a few stress reduction exercises.

V. Relationship of lesson to past and future training

Stress management ties into yesterday's class on handling anger. Many of you mentioned how stressful it is providing "service with a smile" to demanding customers. The anger you feel inside is a definite stressor and needs to be managed in a healthy way. Another stress factor in your job is its fast pace. In tomorrow's class on time management we will discuss several different techniques you can use to get better control of your time.

Body

> *Note:* Use conference method. Have learners generate ideas and record on easel board. Use open-ended questions to encourage discussion. The following items are samples; learners will generate additional ideas. Allow about thirty minutes to discuss items I–IV.

   I. Discuss various causes of stress
     A. Financial pressure
     B. Work pressure
     C. Time constraints
     D.   Family issues
     E. Life changes (can be positive as well as negative; for example, beginning new career)
  II. Discuss perception as a factor in determining stress
     A. External events versus our reaction to them
     B. Sources of feelings

       1. Ourselves
       2. Other people
       3. External event
    C. Any situation can be stress producing. Events are stressors; stress is the reaction.
  III. Identify symptoms of stress
    A. Physical
       1. Digestive upsets
       2. Headaches
       3. Rapid heartbeat
       4. Dry mouth
       5. Insomnia
    B. Emotional and behavioral
       1. Worrying, depression, nightmares
       2. General irritability
       3. Easily upset or discouraged
       4. Frustrated if waiting
       5. Excesses—eating, drinking, sleeping
       6. Difficulty concentrating; memory problems

Note: show videotape at this time.

Note: tell learners to take a break after the videotape and state the time the session will resume.

Note: allow approximately fifty minutes to discuss items IV–VI.

  IV. Solicit learner feedback regarding the videotape
    A. Ask if they have seen similar behaviors in people they know
    B. What is their overall reaction to this videotape?

      C.What were some instances in the videotape of people who seemed to magnify their stress?

V. Identify the effects of unchecked stress

    A. Health problems

    B. Emotional stability

    C.Relationships

VI. Discuss methods for coping with stress

    A. Identify what is stressful for you personally and identify strategies to alleviate

      1. Keep a journal

      2. Reduce demands on yourself

    B. Attitude

      1. Accept reality (for example, realize you can't change other people)

      2. Avoid self-imposed rules such as "I must work hard all the time" or "I must succeed in everything I do"

      3. Stop negative thoughts (such as "it's hopeless" or "I can't win"); practice positive imagery

    C.Improve life skills, such as time management, conflict resolution, relationships skills

    D.   Recreation

    E. Physical activity

      1. Exercise

      2. Relaxation techniques

    F. Maintain a healthy lifestyle

Note: assign a break. State what time the session will resume.

VII. Conduct practice exercise (Annex B)

Note: divide the learners into four separate groups. Have each group work on one of the four case studies found on pages 30–35 of the *Coping with Stress* manual. Each group should review its respective case study and then determine appropriate courses of action that could be taken to cope with the stressful situation described. This exercise will take approximately fifty minutes. Allow twenty minutes for groups to analyze the case and thirty minutes to discuss the four analyses.

Conclusion

I. Ask for final questions or comments

II. Summary

Any situation can lead to stress. Events are the stressors; stress is the reaction. Symptoms of stress vary widely from one person to the next. Too much stress can cause physical as well as emotional problems. Unchecked stress can affect our relationships and even our ability to think clearly. It's important to identify what is stressful to us and to try various coping techniques to find those that are effective.

III. Closing statement

Remember, although we cannot change life's events, we *can* change how we react to them and we *can* effectively cope with stress.

◆ ◆ ◆

Lesson plans are extremely helpful in conducting training. Everything you need to say and do is in front of you in a format that is easy to follow. You can glance down at it periodically to make sure you haven't skipped any points or forgotten to pass out a handout. You don't have to worry if your mind suddenly goes blank and you can't remember the point you were about to make. Because you have planned the sequence for the content, your transitions from one key point to the next will be smooth.

Also, with a planned introduction and closing you are more likely to project confidence even if you're feeling nervous. You may get to the point where you feel you don't really need to reference a particular lesson plan any more but in the meantime you'll be very glad you have it.

PLANNING SHEET 9: LESSON PLAN

Administrative Information

COURSE TITLE

_____

_____

LESSON TITLE

_____

_____

LEARNING OBJECTIVES

_____

_____

_____

_____

_____

_____

_____

_____

_____

_____

PERSONNEL TO BE TRAINED

_____

_____

PREREQUISITES (ESSENTIAL PREVIOUS TRAINING)

_____

_____

_____

TRAINING AIDS, EQUIPMENT AND SUPPLIES

_____

_____

_____

_____

_____

_____

_____

_____

_____

METHOD(S) OF INSTRUCTION

_____

_____

_____

_____

_____

_____

_____

_____

_____

_____

EXAMINATION INFORMATION (DIRECTIONS TO ADMINISTER/SCORE)

_____

_____

_____

_____

_____

_____

_____

_____

_____

REFERENCES

_____

_____

_____

_____

SPECIAL REQUIREMENTS

_____

_____

_____

_____

_____

_____

_____

_____

LESSON PLAN BODY

Introduction

FOCUS ATTENTION ON TOPIC

_____

_____

_____

_____

_____

MOTIVATION

_____

_____

_____

_____

_____

LEARNING OBJECTIVE(S)

_____

_____

_____

_____

_____

_____

_____

_____

_____

OVERVIEW OF LESSON

_____

_____

_____

_____

_____

_____

_____

_____

RELATIONSHIP OF LESSON TO PAST/FUTURE TRAINING

_____

_____

_____

_____

_____

_____

_____

Lesson Content

Topic 1:

      DETAILED OUTLINE OF TOPIC

      ESTIMATED TIME

      INSTRUCTIONS INDICATING WHEN TO USE TRAINING AIDS

      INSTRUCTIONS INDICATING THE TYPE OF METHOD/STRATEGIES/
      TECHNIQUES

      NOTES TO TRAINER

Lesson Content

Topic 2:

      DETAILED OUTLINE OF TOPIC

      ESTIMATED TIME

      INSTRUCTIONS INDICATING WHEN TO USE TRAINING AIDS

      INSTRUCTIONS INDICATING THE TYPE OF METHOD/STRATEGIES/
      TECHNIQUES

      NOTES TO TRAINER

_____

_____

_____

_____

_____

_____

_____

_____

_____

_____

_____

_____

_____

_____

_____

_____

_____

_____

_____

_____

Lesson Content

Topic 3:

DETAILED OUTLINE OF TOPIC

ESTIMATED TIME

INSTRUCTIONS INDICATING WHEN TO USE TRAINING AIDS

INSTRUCTIONS INDICATING THE TYPE OF METHOD/STRATEGIES/
TECHNIQUES

NOTES TO TRAINER

_____

_____

_____

_____

_____

_____

_____

_____

_____

_____

_____

_____

_____

_____

_____

_____

_____

_____

Lesson Content

Topic 4:

       DETAILED OUTLINE OF TOPIC

       ESTIMATED TIME

       INSTRUCTIONS INDICATING WHEN TO USE TRAINING AIDS

       INSTRUCTIONS INDICATING THE TYPE OF METHOD/STRATEGIES/
       TECHNIQUES

       NOTES TO TRAINER

_____

_____

_____

_____

_____

_____

_____

_____

_____

_____

_____

_____

_____

_____

_____

_____

_____

_____

Lesson Content

Topic 5:

       DETAILED OUTLINE OF TOPIC

       ESTIMATED TIME

       INSTRUCTIONS INDICATING WHEN TO USE TRAINING AIDS

       INSTRUCTIONS INDICATING THE TYPE OF METHOD/STRATEGIES/ TECHNIQUES

       NOTES TO TRAINER

_____

_____

_____

_____

_____

_____

_____

_____

_____

_____

_____

_____

_____

_____

_____

_____

_____

_____

Lesson Content

Topic 6:

       DETAILED OUTLINE OF TOPIC

       ESTIMATED TIME

       INSTRUCTIONS INDICATING WHEN TO USE TRAINING AIDS

       INSTRUCTIONS INDICATING THE TYPE OF METHOD/STRATEGIES/ TECHNIQUES

       NOTES TO TRAINER

_____

_____

_____

_____

_____

_____

_____

_____

_____

_____

_____

_____

_____

_____

_____

_____

_____

_____

Lesson Content

Topic 7:

      DETAILED OUTLINE OF TOPIC

      ESTIMATED TIME

      INSTRUCTIONS INDICATING WHEN TO USE TRAINING AIDS

      INSTRUCTIONS INDICATING THE TYPE OF METHOD/STRATEGIES/
      TECHNIQUES

      NOTES TO TRAINER

Conclusion:

FINAL QUESTIONS

_____

_____

_____

SUMMARY

_____

_____

_____

_____

_____

_____

_____

_____

CLOSURE

_____

_____

_____

_____

_____

_____

_____

_____

_____

ANNEX A—PRECLASS ACTIVITY INSTRUCTIONS

_____

_____

_____

_____

_____

_____

_____

_____

_____

_____

_____

_____

_____

_____

_____

_____

_____

_____

_____

_____

_____

_____

_____

_____

_____

_____

_____

ANNEX B—PHOTOCOPIES OF OVERHEAD TRANSPARENCIES

Transparency #1 Title _____

Transparency #2 Title _____

Transparency #3 Title _____

Transparency #4 Title _____

Transparency #5 Title _____

Transparency #6 Title _____

Transparency #7 Title _____

ANNEX C—PHOTOCOPIES OF HANDOUTS

Handout #1 Title _____

Handout #2 Title _____

Handout #3 Title _____

Handout #4 Title _____

Handout #5 Title _____

Handout #6 Title _____

Handout #7 Title _____

ANNEX D—OTHER TRAINING AIDS

35mm slides

_____

_____

_____

_____

_____

_____

_____

_____

Easel charts to be prepared ahead of class

_____

_____

_____

_____

_____

_____

_____

_____

_____

_____

_____

_____

Videotape/audiotape descriptions

_____

_____

_____

_____

_____

_____

_____

_____

_____

_____

_____

_____

_____

_____

Computer slide show description

_____

_____

_____

_____

_____

_____

_____

_____

_____

_____

_____

_____

ANNEX E—PHOTOCOPIES OF PRACTICE EXERCISES

Includes directions on how to administer and answer key or other means to provide learners' feedback

ANNEX F—PHOTOCOPIES OF TESTS

Includes directions on how to administer and answer key or other means to provide learners' feedback

CHAPTER TEN

EVALUATING TRAINING EFFECTIVENESS

The Dog and the Shell

Once there was a Dog who loved to eat eggs. One day when he was especially hungry, he spied a big pile of white oyster shells in a basket on the kitchen table. Thinking they were eggs, his mouth watered at the thought of eating them. He leaped up on the table, grabbed the largest shell and gulped it down as fast as he could. Soon he had the worst bellyache he had ever known and began to howl with pain. After realizing his mistake, he said, "Where did I ever get the idea that everything that's round is an egg?" They who act without sufficient thought will often fall into unsuspected danger.

Effective trainers solicit and use feedback to evaluate the instruction they offer. However, they must be able to distinguish the shells from the eggs before making changes based on the feedback they receive.

Evaluation is a broad term that means collecting information for the purpose of decision making. At a minimum, it is important to know that the learning objectives were met. Also, professional trainers seek continually to improve the training they offer. They must collect information that enables them to do so. There are three broad sources of information available for the evaluation of training: the learners, the trainer, and persons outside the training environment. You must decide the type of information you wish to collect and when you will collect it.

Learner Feedback

The learners are the major source of information for determining whether the learning objectives were achieved. Additionally, they can provide invaluable information regarding their reactions to the training. They will often offer excellent suggestions for improvements that would never have occurred to you had you not solicited their comments.

Were the learning objectives met? The learning objectives you wrote were road maps leading to specific outcomes. How can you be sure you have reached the desired destination? The only way you will know is to test the learners. A test does not have to be formal and does not have to be graded. Most training "tests" are activities the trainer has constructed that require the learners to perform the learning objectives. These are referred to as performance tests. For example, if the learning objectives include the ability to create a graph using a given computer software program, the learners would each be required to construct a graph. For "soft" skills, the trainer can create real-life scenarios that require the learners to apply the concepts discussed in the training. For example, a new supervisors' course can include mini-case studies that require a decision to be made or problem to be solved. Each learner could individually outline a course of action and then the group could discuss the various alternatives and the possible pros and cons associated with them. Similarly, after a lesson on interviewing techniques, each learner could practice interviewing another learner or possibly the trainer.

Do not wait until the training is nearly completed to give performance tests. It is important to identify any learning problems early so that a learner does not become lost to the point where it is too late to master the learning objectives. Therefore, if the training is lengthy or complex, use a separate test for each major topic or skill. Note: when assigning a performance test, look to see if any learners appear uncertain how to proceed. If so, approach them and offer individualized assistance.

Verbal Feedback

It takes a great deal of courage to solicit feedback from the learners about their reactions to the training. You are opening yourself up to possible criticism and that is certainly an uncomfortable and anxious feeling. However, being an ostrich will do little to further your professional development or the improvement of any future training you may conduct. I have found that most people offer helpful feedback when asked. I encourage you not to wait until the end of the session to solicit feedback. It is certainly appropriate to obtain feedback then, but this should not be the only time you seek it. Before you get too far along in the session, say something like, "I'd like to get your reaction to the training so far. Is it useful? Do you have any suggestions for me?" My experience has been that learners really appreciate being asked and offer helpful comments.

If you used a preclass activity that involved eliciting individual goals and expectations, refer back to the items listed and ask if the expectations are being met so far. Listen to the comments with an open mind. Often a minor change on your part can make a major change in the way the learners perceive the training. Of course, each situation is different and you may or may not be in a position to implement a given suggestion. Sometimes just listening to their concerns is helpful even if there is little you can do to address them. If the training length is more than one day, solicit verbal feedback more than once before the end of the session. When you do reach the end of the session, give everyone an opportunity to comment on the session. Again, refer back to the pre-class activity if applicable.

Written Feedback

Most trainers use some type of evaluation form at the end of the training. Some choose to pass out evaluation forms at the beginning of the training and ask learners to complete the relevant sections as the training progresses. I have not found much difference in the amount of written feedback I receive either way. I have found that most learners do not care to complete elaborate evaluation forms and that it is best to keep forms to no more than one page in length. The reverse side of the form can be used for learners to write comments. When constructing your own evaluation form, decide specifically what type of information you wish to collect. Listed below are typical areas addressed on training evaluation forms.

- Training objectives clearly stated
- Clarity of explanations
- Ability to check for learner comprehension
- Ability to diagnose and correct learning difficulties
- Feedback given to learners
- Knowledge of subject
- Organization of material (logical sequence)
- Level of training (not too elementary or too complex)
- New terms explained
- Examples realistic
- Key points stressed
- Unnecessary detail minimized
- Questions encouraged
- Questions thoroughly answered
- Involvement of learners
- Quality of training aids (visible, relevant to objective)

- Amount of material covered in allotted time (too much-too little)
- Trainer enthusiasm
- Trainer responsive to learner concerns
- Trainer provides individual assistance to learners as needed
- Pace of instruction (not too slow or too fast)
- Verbal skills (volume, rate of speech, inflection, fluency)
- Nonverbal skills (eye contact, facial expression, gestures, movement)
- Listening skills of trainer
- Ability to maintain learner interest
- Evidence of preparation
- Physical facilities

These areas can be addressed in different ways. You may wish to have learners give a numerical rating to the selected items, perhaps a scale of one to five with one being poor and five excellent. A sample of this format appears on page 168.

(*Note:* some trainers prefer numerical ratings that do not allow for a neutral rating such as a three on a scale of one to five. They want learners to indicate if they feel generally more positive or negative. Therefore, they would use a different numbering system such as rating on a scale of one to four.) When using numerical ratings, be sure it's clear what the numbers indicate.

Instead of using a numerical rating, some evaluation forms give learners choices for each item such as very effective, somewhat effective, or not effective, or simply okay or not okay. A sample of this format appears on page 169. Usually there is a small box next to each choice for the learner to check.

Another option is to construct statements and have learners indicate the extent to which they agree (strongly agree, agree, neither agree nor disagree, disagree, strongly disagree). A sample of this format appears on page 170. For example: "The training gave me ideas that will help me perform my job more effectively."

If you are not going to fill the entire page with specific items to be addressed, you may wish to include a few open-ended questions that do not require a lengthy response—for example, "What did you find most valuable?" or "What changes would you make?" Another alternative is to draw a couple of lines to be used to write comments beneath each item.

Interpreting Learner Feedback

You will find that each group of learners has its own idiosyncrasies. Your professional judgment must also come into play before you adopt a particular suggestion. I recall one particular group that adamantly insisted that a particular change was needed. I did not make it. When I conducted the same training for numerous other groups, that particular suggestion never surfaced again. Unless you have overwhelming evidence of the need to do so, look for trends or patterns of comments among different groups of learners before you make major revisions to the training. When you are conducting the same training for different groups over a long period of time, it is possible that one particular group of learners will be atypical. This can occur for a variety of reasons. One group may have a more extensive background in the subject. Perhaps one group was forced to attend the training by its supervisor whereas the other groups of learners requested the training. Variances like these will also result in contradictory suggestions coming from the same group, as when one learner says the course needs to be shortened and another learner says it needs to be lengthened. It is important to validate comments over time, keeping in mind the typical background of the learners who attend the training.

This principle of validation also applies to individual learners who make extreme comments. Perhaps the evaluation forms you receive indicate a positive response overall. Let's say on a scale of one to five most items are checked either four or five. However, only one of the forms contains any written comments and this particular form is extremely critical of the training. It contains broad comments such as,

"This training was a complete waste of my time. The entire session could have been easily completed in one day instead of five." Comments such as these need to be considered in the context of both the group and the individual making them. First of all, although extreme, this is the only negative response you received. Second, sweeping comments such as the training being a "complete waste of time" are rarely accurate. It's highly unlikely that everything about the training was worthless. It's more likely that this learner is angry about something in particular and is using the evaluation form as a vehicle to vent that anger. You may or may not be able to find out the true source of discontentment. If the evaluation form was not anonymous, you may try talking to the learner to see if you can get more specific information.

I recall an instance in which a learner wrote an extremely hostile evaluation. I later learned that she was angry because she had been forced to attend the course, had attended a similar course in the past so the information was not new to her, and had wanted to go on vacation the week the course was in session and was extremely upset at missing the vacation. I recall another instance in which a learner wrote a highly critical evaluation of a group dynamics course. This particular learner was very domineering in nature. During the course, his domineering behavior was challenged by other learners. I believe that the negative evaluation was an outlet for his anger over not being able to control others the way he had been accustomed to doing in the past.

You will develop a better framework for validating learner feedback with experience. Although it's important to keep an open mind, it's also important to realize that not all feedback is necessarily useful.

Self-Evaluation

Get in the habit of reflecting on what happened during the training at the end of each day. Jot down notes regarding how things went. What seemed to go well? What seemed not to go well? How was the time factor—was it considerably over or under the amount of time planned? Did the learners react very differently than you expected? If so, in what way? Did the learners seem confused during any part of the training? What was the level of participation? Did the learners seem bored? What do you think you would do differently the next time you conduct this training? A few minutes of reflection will result in ideas to continually improve your programs.

Other Resources

The learners are not the only people in a position to help you analyze training effectiveness. Other staff may have additional information. The person who actually coordinated the training session (usually someone from the company's human resources department) often receives feedback from the learners. Touch base with this person before you leave and ask if he or she has any feedback for you. If the training has clear on-the-job applications, the learners' supervisors are in the position to determine if the learners are applying the training on the job. You may wish to call them or send out short surveys (with self-addressed stamped envelopes) after the learners have been back on the job long enough to begin transferring what they have learned to the job. Finally, other experienced trainers are a great resource. It may be possible to have another trainer observe you the first time you present a training session. This person can provide moral support as well as specific suggestions. If that's not possible, try contacting someone who has conducted similar training in your field for advice. Local chapters of professional associations such as the American Society for Training and Development (ASTD) are a good resource if you don't personally know anyone you might call.

WORKSHOP EVALUATION

LEGEND: 5 = EXCELLENT, 4 = VERY GOOD, 3 = GOOD, 2 = FAIR, 1 = POOR

Please rate the following aspects of the workshop.

Training objectives clearly stated	5 4 3 2 1
Clarity of explanations	5 4 3 2 1
Level of difficulty	5 4 3 2 1
Audio/Visuals	5 4 3 2 1
Learner participation	5 4 3 2 1
Questions thoroughly answered	5 4 3 2 1
Pace (not too slow or too fast)	5 4 3 2 1
Trainer enthusiasm	5 4 3 2 1
Trainer responsive to learner concerns	5 4 3 2 1
Physical facilities	5 4 3 2 1

What did you like best about the workshop?

What suggestions do you have for making the workshop more effective?

Thank you!

RATING FORM

Please take a few moments to respond to the items below. Your feedback will be very helpful for future course revisions.

Application of Training to My Job

___Very Effective   ___Somewhat Effective   ___Not Effective

Clarity of Explanations

___Very Effective   ___Somewhat Effective   ___Not Effective

Workshop Materials

___Very Effective   ___Somewhat Effective   ___Not Effective

Involvement of Learners

___Very Effective   ___Somewhat Effective   ___Not Effective

Use of Audio/Visuals

___Very Effective   ___Somewhat Effective   ___Not Effective

Methods of Instruction

___Very Effective   ___Somewhat Effective   ___Not Effective

Pace of Instruction

___Very Effective   ___Somewhat Effective   ___Not Effective

Trainer's Communication Skills

___Very Effective   ___Somewhat Effective   ___Not Effective

Please write any comments on the reverse side of this form.

Thank you!

LEARNER QUESTIONNAIRE

Please indicate if you agree or disagree with the following statements by circling one of the choices listed.

The training will help me perform my job more effectively.

Strongly Agree   Agree   Neither Agree Nor Disagree   Disagree   Strongly Disagree

Comments:

The time was used efficiently.

Strongly Agree   Agree   Neither Agree Nor Disagree   Disagree   Strongly Disagree

Comments:

The training was clear and easy to follow.

Strongly Agree   Agree   Neither Agree Nor Disagree   Disagree   Strongly Disagree

Comments:

The practice exercises were helpful.

Strongly Agree   Agree   Neither Agree Nor Disagree   Disagree   Strongly Disagree

Comments:

The trainer encouraged questions.

Strongly Agree   Agree   Neither Agree Nor Disagree   Disagree   Strongly Disagree

Comments:

The trainer provided individual assistance to learners as needed.

Strongly Agree   Agree   Neither Agree Nor Disagree   Disagree   Strongly Disagree

Comments:

Please use the reverse side of this form for any additional comments you may have.

Thank you!

INDEX

More resources from Jossey-Bass/Pfeiffer

Create customized, effective new-employee orientations

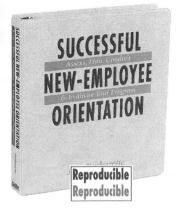

Successful New-Employee Orientation
Assess, Plan, Conduct, and Evaluate Your Program

Jean Barbazette

The most common complaints about new-employee orientation are that it is boring and overwhelming or that nothing happens and the new person is left to "sink or swim." The result is often a confused new employee who is not productive and is likely to leave the organization within a year! Your orientation needs to be a planned welcome that reaffirms your hiring decision.

Use this resource to meet orientation objectives such as:

- **Providing** critical information and resources in a timely manner
- **Making** the new employee independently productive quickly
- **Helping** the new employee feel secure and get off to a good start by understanding your organization's culture

This comprehensive resource will help you design or revise an orientation program that is effective and full of variety. It includes suggestions for the timely delivery of information and is filled with everything you need to create your customized orientation program: checklists, examples, sample letters, activities, and evaluation forms. An added bonus is a full section on orienting temporary employees!

Learn how to assess your orientation needs, select the appropriate content, implement that program, and evaluate its success. Even if you're a novice, these user-friendly materials will help you create a dynamic, effective orientation program.

Successful New-Employee Orientation / **Code 04179** / 128 pages / looseleaf / **$89.95**

How to Write Training Materials

Linda Stoneall

This book will help you translate your training expertise into simple, effective prose for adult education.

Get helpful tips on designing materials that:

- **Contain** enough detail for accuracy
- **Enable** people with limited knowledge to conduct training
- **Promote** trainers' consistency and accountability
- **Enhance** participation and transfer of learning

Use this book as a guide to improve the quality of your training materials. Then turn to individual chapters for help when writing research questions, learning activities, training designs, participant handouts, video scripts, and more!

How to Write Training Materials / **Code 11526** / 150 pages / paperbound / **$29.95**

A Handbook of Job Aids

Allison Rossett & Jeannette Gautier-Downes

Job aids make it easier to perform tasks by providing access to information, pro-cedures, policies, and examples. Paired with training and supervisory support, job aids play a key role in the introduction of new work technologies and systems.

In this book, the authors present job aids that expand on these traditional uses. They include job aids that coach perspectives and decisions (such as on-line help systems and performance support tools). Order today!

A Handbook of Job Aids / **Code 697** / 195 pages / hardbound / **$39.95**

More resources from Jossey-Bass/Pfeiffer

More resources from Jossey-Bass/Pfeiffer

"A must-read for anyone who wants training to be effective and engaging."

—Sivasailam Thiagarajan, author, Games by Thiagi

Active Training
A Handbook of Techniques, Designs, Case Examples, and Tips

Mel Silberman

One of the most comprehensive texts on training ever compiled, *Active Training* shows you how to teach adults the way they learn best: by doing. It will help you effectively design and conduct experientially based training programs in public- and private-sector organizations—whether you are a novice trainer or seasoned professional.

This handbook is packed with information to help you create new training programs, modify existing courses, and combine a variety of facilitation techniques to conduct any training program more successfully. It includes over 200 designs and case examples drawn from more than 45 training professionals.

It leads you through:

- Assessing the training group
- Developing training objectives
- Using experiential learning approaches
- Conducting presentations and discussions
- Planning, designing, and sequencing training activities
- Providing for "back-on-the job" application
- Gaining leadership of a training group
- Concluding and evaluating training programs

Active Training is a complete guide to experiential learning techniques, illustrated by hundreds of examples. Use it to enhance all your training interventions.

"Silberman's book proves that learning can be fun. Its usable, practical ideas make training come alive!"

—Edward E. Scannell, coauthor, Games Trainers Play series

101 Ways to Make Training Active

Mel Silberman

These proven, generic activities will enliven your sessions and deepen learning and retention—no matter what you're teaching.

This active training field guide provides activities useful for:

- Involving participants
- Promoting back-on-the-job application
- Facilitating team learning
- Reviewing program content
- Developing skills . . . and more!

You'll also get 160 training tips about: • meeting participant expectations • regaining control of the group • making lectures active • forming groups ... and more!

Easily slip any of these 101 strategies into any training you are conducting and watch your training come alive!

Contents

The Nuts and Bolts of Active Training: 160 Tips • How to Get Active Participation from the Start • Team-Building Strategies • On-the-Spot Assessment Strategies • Immediate Learning Involvement Strategies • How to Teach Information, Skills, and Attitudes Actively • Full-Class Learning • Stimulating Discussion • Prompting Questions • Team Learning • Peer Teaching • Independent Learning • Effective Learning • Skill Development • How to Make Training Unforgettable • Reviewing Strategies • Self-Assessment • Application Planning • Final Sentiments • Index to Case Examples

Active Training / **Code 09084** / 284 pages / hardbound / **$44.95**

101 Ways to Make Training Active / **Code 04756** / 304 pages / paperbound / **$39.95**

CALL FREE: 800.274.4434 · FAX FREE: 800.569.0443

More resources from Jossey-Bass/Pfeiffer

Advanced training designs prepare teams for future responsibilities

Team Building for the Future
Beyond the Basics

Robin L. Elledge & Steven L. Phillips

This comprehensive, team building resource provides you with the right information and training designs to help you tackle specific issues or overcome difficulties that today's teams face. These training designs help you intervene effectively with:

- Trustless teams
- Teams in chaos
- Temporary task teams
- Merged teams
- And more!

The customizable training designs are complete with activities, objectives, and guidelines, plus handout, flip chart content, and overhead masters. This resource

also introduces a new model of team effectiveness and is most useful if you already have fundamental group-process and team building skills.

Make the effects of your next team intervention long-lasting with the guidance of *Team Building for the Future*.

The all-in-one resource to execute team-building programs

The Team-Building Source Book
Steven L. Phillips & Robin L. Elledge

Here is everything you need to lead a group through team-building! You can help a group accomplish specific, basic tasks necessary for productive work. Plus, you can adapt each module as needed to meet your group's unique circumstances.

This handy, looseleaf volume gives you instructions, reproducible handouts, information for flip charts, samples of assessment materials, and complete coverage of the team-building process! Includes 11 complete interventions that address basic team needs such as: • clarifying roles • conflict management • problem solving • and more.

Each section covers a different phase:

- **Getting** started
- **Collecting** the data
- **Analyzing** the data
- **Giving** feedback
- **Implementing** goals
- **Follow-up**

The Team-Building Source Book can be followed phase by phase or used as a reference. Either way, it's a valuable resource to help you design and facilitate successful team-building sessions!

More resources from Jossey-Bass/Pfeiffer

Earthquake Survival
Activity and Leader's Guide

Here's a fun "situation" to help your teams quickly improve their groups' functioning. Immediately your participants will learn functional skills that will improve their performance in the workplace.

Enjoy variety and flexibility with these three complete activities:

• "Earthquake Survival Situations" Quiz • "Things to Have" to Prepare for an Earthquake • "Things to Do" During and Immediately After an Earthquake.

The *Leader's Guide* includes instructions for administering the activities and conducting discussions, possible variations, lecturettes, and samples of all forms and handouts.

Lost at Sea
Simulation and Leader's Manual

In this classic simulation, participants work individually, then as a group, to assess 15 items salvaged from a yachting accident, based on their value for survival. Results are compared with the expert rankings supplied by the U.S. Merchant Marines. Through self-scoring, the group immediately sees how well they performed.

The *Leader's Manual* offers instructions for facilitating the activity.

In this simulation, a group is stranded on a rubber life raft with minimal supplies including: • Fishing kit • Mosquito netting • Shark repellant • Shaving mirror • Two chocolate bars • And 10 other items.

Wilderness Survival
Simulation and Leader's Manual

This survival activity poses 12 situations that someone lost in a wilderness might encounter—snakes, bears, an early snow, and other potentially life-threatening scenarios. Participants make individual then group decisions about how to survive each situation. These decisions are compared with those of expert naturalists.

The *Leader's Manual* offers instructions for facilitating the activity.

There are many life-threatening encounters in this mythical wilderness. How well will your group work together to survive?

Earthquake Survival Activities / **Code 04519** / 24 pages / paperbound / **$9.95**

Leader's Guide / **Code 04500** / 48 pages / paperbound / **$17.95**

Lost at Sea Simulation / **Code 89S** / 7 pages / **$6.95**

Leader's Manual / **Code 543** / 10 pages / **$17.95**

Wilderness Survival Simulation / **Code 89R** / 10 pages / **$6.95**

Leader's Manual / **Code 541** / 10 pages / **$17.95**

CALL FREE: **800.274.4434** • FAX FREE: **800.569.0443**

More resources from Jossey-Bass/Pfeiffer